C0-AUY-479

THE EARLIEST YEARS

The Growth and Development of Children under Five

BY

O. M. WOODWARD, M.A.

*Senior Lecturer in Education at the
Froebel Educational Institute*

THE QUEEN'S AWARD
TO INDUSTRY 1966

PERGAMON PRESS

OXFORD · LONDON · EDINBURGH · NEW YORK
TORONTO · SYDNEY · PARIS · BRAUNSCHWEIG

Pergamon Press Ltd., Headington Hill Hall, Oxford
4 & 5 Fitzroy Square, London W.1

Pergamon Press (Scotland) Ltd., 2 & 3 Teviot Place, Edinburgh 1

Pergamon Press Inc., 44–01 21st Street, Long Island City, New York 11101

Pergamon of Canada, Ltd., 207 Queen's Quay West, Toronto 1

Pergamon Press (Aust.) Pty. Ltd., Rushcutters Bay, Sydney, New South Wales

Pergamon Press S.A.R.L., 24 rue des Ecoles, Paris 5e

Vieweg & Sohn GmbH, Burgplatz 1, 33 Braunschweig

Printed in Great Britain by A. Wheaton & Co., Exeter

Contents

v

Introduction. Comparison between the newborn baby and the five-year-old. The helplessness of the newborn baby. The acquired skills of the five-year-old.

MOST psychologists are agreed that the first five years of life are the most important. This period is the most vital in the formation of personality, and once this pattern of development is set it can only be changed with difficulty. In these years he develops in himself the traits of confidence and security or of fear and insecurity. He also develops attitudes towards other people which are going to make him socially acceptable or anti-social and unacceptable. His first primitive concepts of spiritual, moral and social values are formed from the way in which he is treated and from the ways in which he sees other people behave. By the enormous number of new experiences through which he passes, his first approach to intellectual learning is made. He also learns physically, through constant trial, leading to success or failure, how to use his body to its fullest potential. He learns to control his muscles and limbs; to learn their fullest use and to learn to co-ordinate between them. These first five years of his life are a vital time for all aspects of learning.

If we look at a tiny newborn baby and compare him with an alert energetic five-year-old, we begin to realise how much the newborn child has to learn; how much he has to experience of difficulties and of successes and failures, in order to come so far in so short a time. When we look at this baby, however, we must remember that he has in most cases had already nine months of life and during those nine months a tremendous amount of growth and development has taken place. It is important, therefore, to remember that in the case of a prematurely born baby his stage of development may be as much as two months behind his own normal point of development at birth. He is not backward or retarded, but is at his proper stage of his own developmental pattern. Although there are differences of opinion about the amount and character of the influences on the child of ante-natal experiences, there is general agreement that they are important and are very varied from one individual to another. The mother's health and personality and the physical environment of the home are all bound to have an effect on the unborn child.

The baby, although he may appear, in comparison with the five-year-old, to be so incapable and helpless, is yet able to do a great deal towards his own successful development in life. The change from the ante-natal conditions to those in the outside world is a tremendous one and therefore the first period of the baby's life is one of adjustment. Although he is physiologically ready to function, he has to establish a stable level in such operations as breathing, circulation, the taking in of food and digesting it ; in the elimination of waste products and in the regulation of body temperatures.

The parts of the brain have developed at different rates so that some are more advanced than others. Those parts which control the physiological processes and the automatic reflex actions are relatively more developed than the upper brain centres. The reflex actions of the very young baby show how far he has developed in the maturation of the brain. He already has a well-developed set of patterns of behaviour which are adaptable to the new environmental conditions which must be met successfully for him to survive outside his mother's body.

His senses also are ready so that they can function when he has reached the right point in his maturation. His eyes have sensitivity, but there is doubt as to whether he can as yet perceive objects, and he finds it impossible to focus. It is doubtful whether in the first few days there is much hearing of any kind, but this same hearing quickly becomes very acute and sensitive. The sense of taste is also present, but he probably has not yet learnt to appreciate differences of flavour. He has also a sense of smell, but this again is probably not well developed at birth.

The sense of touch is developed before birth and is most important for the development and learning of the baby. His first contact with the world outside is through the skin. His first reaction to being touched is a general diffuse response, not specific in any way, since he seems to have little ability to recognise the source of the stimulus. His first learning comes through the sense of touch. The recognition of the source of his food, through touch, the feeling of warmth to his skin and bodily discomfort of any kind are all aspects of his learning which must take place for his survival and development.

Although all babies are similar in some respects in their stage of development at birth, each one is unique and there are great differences between them. This is shown by their patterns of behaviour. Some children, for instance, have much longer and deeper periods of sleep ; others lie awake quietly while others cry far more when they are awake. In the same way their emotional behaviour is different, one from another. At this early stage emotional response is more in the nature of general excitement. The response is one of the infant's whole body, whether it is stimulated by the inner need of such factors as hunger, or from the outer stimulation of physical discomfort of too much heat or cold. Some infants are more easily excited than others and in some cases the reaction is much more violent. Even at this age they show quickly the pattern of personality emerging.

The baby, then, is well equipped even at birth to start his life and development in the outside world, but he is still very helpless in comparison with the five-year-old child. Everything externally has to be done for him. He cannot raise his head ; he cannot sit or stand and he cannot get from place to place. His eyes cannot focus properly and he cannot see anything clearly. The movements of his limbs are random, jerky, and apparently without purposeful motivation. He has no method of communication with other people except his general cry of distress. His feelings of contentment are not yet actively expressed and his social development is, as far as we know, non-existent. He has been completely protected from all first-hand experiences of the world, so that he has no concepts and he has no language in which to express them. He has no emotional feelings towards other people. He does not love them and he does not hate them, and he has no awareness of himself as a personality with interactions with other personalities. He is not " good " or " bad ". He is a-moral, without any moral, spiritual or social ideas or values.

Everything therefore in connection with the outside world has to be learned by the newborn baby, and this includes all aspects of his development. Learning is so often thought of only as intellectual learning which helps one to pass examinations. The learning on the physical side, on the emotional side, and on the social and spiritual sides is quite as important if the child is to become a successful adult or even a successful five-year-old. Although in comparison with that of animals, human childhood is a very prolonged period, yet in comparison with all that he has to learn it is a very short time. He will do more intensive learning during these first five years than at any other period of his life, and therefore he will need as much help and encouragement as he can get in order to achieve that successful development.

If we now look at a group of happy five-year-olds and compare them with the newborn baby, we will see how far they have developed and how much they have learned in so short a time. In the first place there are great individual differences. Although babies differ physically in weight and in length of body and limbs, these differences are by the age of five much accentuated. Some are taller ; some are smaller ; some are thinner and some are fatter. Some have greater ease and ability in movement, and some have much greater muscle control and co-ordination than others. Each individual child has a unique and particular complex of growth, but at the same time there is a similar pattern of progression of growth for all. At five years old, therefore, although one would be aware that some children have progressed more quickly or more slowly than others, one would see on the whole a general pattern of development. By this time they have nearly lost the top-heaviness of earlier childhood, so that they no longer have to put out their arms to balance themselves, and they can get up and down off the floor with more ease. The average five-year-old is now less chubby and is losing the baby fat, and his head is beginning to be more in proportion to the rest of his body. In the same way he is losing the " pot-belly " and the curved spine of the toddler and manages to stand in a more erect position. He has much more control over his limbs and certain movements have become so habitual to him that he does them automatically. Thus sitting, standing, walking and running are no longer the hesitant, tentative movements which might succeed or might fail ; success is now taken for granted. The five-year-old is, however, still in the stage of finding pleasure and satisfaction in movement for its own sake. He will run happily round the playground in school ; get up and sit down for the sheer delight in the movement, while at the same time, without being aware of it, he is perfecting his skills in movement. Thus he has learned to run accurately where he wants to go, and is learning to take an angle while he is still running, where before he tended to move in a curve. Although he may still stumble, trip and fall, this is usually because his mind is on other things, not because his movement is unsuccessful as in earlier years. His movements are becoming more economical and therefore he can do more in a shorter time. His ankle and leg muscles are stronger so that he is beginning to lose the flat-footed walk of the younger child. He can jump and climb with confidence and hang upside-down on parallel bars supported only by his legs, and he gains confidence in his abilities by so doing. He is moving more rhythmically and with more " flow ", although at times his movements may still be more jerky and uncontrolled as at a younger stage, particularly if he is emotionally disturbed about anything. On the whole he has not yet acquired enough hand–eye co-ordination to catch a ball accurately, but he throws one with confidence, quite often in the right direction.

In smaller, more delicate, movements also he is beginning to show progress. He can now handle a paint brush in an adult manner, no longer in the overhand grasp, and he uses his wrist and hand instead of his whole arm and shoulder. He can put the paint on the paper where he wants it to go, and although on the whole he still uses large sweeping movements, he will at times use the brush to make more delicate lines, dots and circles. With a pencil also he still prefers a large free movement and finds difficulty in copying accurately letters and figures put before him by the teacher—he has not usually reached this stage of maturity.

He delights in using bricks for building and will place them just where he wants them even though this involves very difficult balancing of one on top of another. At the same time he still enjoys the big and more uncontrolled movement of knocking down what he has built when he has no further use for it. He can use a large needle which has been threaded for him to make large stitches in cloth, going in no particular direction, and can so manipulate a shoe-lace as to thread large beads on it. He can use scissors to cut with, though he still has difficulty in keeping to a cutting line. He can use a small blunt-ended saw to cut soft wood in the direction he wants to cut, and hammer in a nail where he wants it to go. His hand and finger muscles have become strong enough to manipulate clay with ease, and he can use it now successfully to produce articles like balls or " sausages " if he has had previous experience in prodding and pounding and experimenting with the material. He will use sand to produce sand-pies or castles or tunnels, and can pour water accurately and without spilling from one container to another. He can cut out pictures and pieces of material and paste them on to a large piece of paper in order to make a collage picture and can stick together all kinds of scrap materials to produce a model of something he knows, like an aeroplane, car, bus or ship.

But with all these creative materials he may at any given time revert to the earlier ways of experimenting with the material and of finding out about its properties, in what may seem to us, a haphazard way.

He has by now acquired many of the skills of day to day living so that he can with a little help dress himself, fasten his buttons and zip-fasteners, although he may still find difficulty with buckles and shoe-laces. He can wash himself, and with some supervision can make attempts at combing and brushing his hair. He can go to the toilet by himself and no longer needs adult prompting and supervision. He can feed himself and can manage a small knife and fork without difficulty.

In the social and emotional aspects of his development the five-year-old has made tremendous progress towards living in society. He is beginning to live with other people as equals. He is beginning to be a personality in his own right and to show traits of character and personality which reflect those of the members of his family, so that his mother may say that he " is just like his father " or that " he takes after my family ; they all have quick tempers ". He is still egocentric and he cannot yet put himself in the place of anybody else. He is still, to himself, the most important person in his world. What he says and does is obviously right to him and he cannot see why everybody else does not think so also. However, he has come far from the rather negative attitude of the three-year-old, when " no " was his favourite word, and he is beginning to accept that he must do as he is told even though he may not approve of it. He still needs to be given a short and explicit reason for his obedience. He finds it difficult to accept the fact that he is ever wrong and has to be helped over his failures because these lower his estimation of himself and of his own powers. He is, however, just beginning to accept that there are modes and patterns of behaviour which are acceptable to other people, not only those of his mother, although these patterns may be different from hers. He is still largely dependent on her, as she still represents to him his basic security ; the person to whom he may safely return from school.

At the same time he is beginning to accept and welcome the help and friendliness of other adults outside the home circle, and because these relationships are more impersonal and less emotionally involved than that with his mother, he often appears to be more obedient and co-operative in school than he is at home. Mothers are sometimes distressed because their children are so " good " at school, and so " naughty " at home, but this is often the measure of security that the child feels in his own home. He knows unconsciously that however difficult he may be at home he will never lose his mother's love, whereas in school the adults, particularly at first, are rather unknown and unpredictable factors. He is not sure of their abiding relationship with him, and therefore this relationship, although it may appear to be very good, and often is, will still not have nearly as much effect on the child in later life as that with his mother. He likes helping his mother around the house and loves to be made responsible for a job, and where he has found success in such jobs, he will be ready to help the teacher in his classroom in the same way. This helps him to take his place in the society of the school.

At the same time as he is coming to grips with an adult world outside the home, by the time he is five he is beginning to make a real relationship with children of his own age. This is usually only in small groups of two or three children. He has not yet reached the " gang " stage of the Junior School child and quite often a group will last only for a short time. The relationship veers very quickly from friendliness and co-operation to anger and aggressive behaviour, and the children still need adult help to smooth over difficulties and to re-establish friendly play. The child still finds it difficult, because of his natural egocentricity, to share toys with other children or to give anything of his own away, but he is beginning to find that to be " unselfish " gains him adult approval. He no longer, or very rarely, throws a temper tantrum when he is frustrated in any way, as he did at an earlier stage of development, but he is beginning to translate his feelings of aggression into language, rather than into hitting, kicking, biting or screaming.

When he calls his mother names, it may be distressing for her and she may be embarrassed if it happens in public, but it is a tremendous step forward from the earlier manifestations of anger in a physical form. At this time he has a very great admiration for his father and tries to model himself on him. He will boast wildly about his father's capabilities and will indulge in fantastic stories about his prowess. Nothing is too difficult for his " Dad " ; he can do anything.

On the intellectual side also he has reached a high stage of development in comparison with the newborn baby. Individual differences between children in this respect may be very great, since their early experiences may have been very different. Most children, however, have had a great number of first-hand experiences from which they have formed a vast number of mental concepts, although they may not understand these concepts at the adult level of understanding. The child of five has acquired a wide vocabulary and although he is not always accurate in the adult use of words, this language ability helps him to organise his concepts and to begin to think more rationally and logically. The " logic " is very childish and therefore sometimes incomprehensible to adults, but one can see the beginnings of a real reasoning process in the way that the child shows that he can make relations between experiences, both practical and verbal, and make comparisons and contrasts between them. He is beginning to make inferences from his experiences and to foresee what may happen. For example, he will know that if he pours water from a large container into a smaller one, the water will overflow. He has, however, not yet reached the stage of abstract thought, so that number symbols, either verbal or written, have no real meaning for him as such. He may use number words glibly ; count up to ten or twenty, and recognise number symbols, but the manipulation of numbers in sums is usually beyond his comprehension. He will in his play have many valuable number experiences on which he will later base the real abstract understanding. This apparent understanding is often most deceptive to parents and teachers, and therefore we may demand too much from the child, not realising how little understanding he has. This is quite probably the cause of the dislike that many children have for mathematics in later school years. In the same way that the child does the numerical naming he may name colours correctly and yet in his own painting he will quite happily paint a yellow daffodil purple or red. He still paints as he thinks and not as he sees, and he has not yet made the relationship between verbalisation of experiences and his own creative experiences, although he is beginning to do so.

The child at this age is intensely interested in all natural phenomena. He is aware of light and dark, thunder and lightning, wind and rain and snow. He wants to know about all living things, plants and animals and insects. Nothing is distasteful or frightening to him unless he has been conditioned to fear things, like spiders, by his mother's fear of them. He is continually asking questions and his constant " how " and " why " and " when " sometimes become exasperating to the adult. He has got beyond the earlier stage of asking questions for the sake of practising speech or of getting attention, and really wants an answer and will pursue an inquiry until he gets that answer. The child of five is interested in how everything works and sometimes gets into trouble for taking things to pieces and hence " being destructive ". He has not yet acquired the ability to form spatial concepts, though the very beginnings of these are apparent in his paintings. He will therefore find great difficulty in attempting to learn to read, although he enjoys looking at books, both pictures and printing, and he will repeat a story from memory, pretending to read it from a book. His memory at this stage is very good indeed and therefore adults are often deceived by the child's apparent ability to read. The ability to differentiate between the shapes of words and letters, to compare and contrast them, however, has not usually developed by this age. His imagination is strong and vivid and he plays continually in phantasy games, either alone or with companions. He plays out imaginatively experiences which he does not understand and so comes to a greater clarification of ideas concerning the world around him which he has tried in vain to understand in reality.

The child at five is a naturally rhythmic animal and so he likes to have musical experiences. He can differentiate between high and low pitch. He can hold a rhythm and move to it or beat it on a percussion instrument or recognise a familiar rhythm when it is played to him. He can follow in movement different moods in music, quick and slow, jerky and smooth, and uses his whole body in interpretation. This interpretation is at his own level, however, and he should not yet be expected to accept adult-imposed movements. If these are forced upon him too soon he will lose his own creative natural impulses in music and gradually become bored with school music and will find his outlet in the " pop " music which he hears constantly at home. He can learn many songs easily and can approximate to a tune, though here again individual differences are very great. He finds such enjoyment in singing, however, whether in or out of tune, that he should be encouraged at all times. He has as yet not much concept of space, but is beginning to understand the real meanings of high and low, wide and narrow, and in his paintings he is beginning to place the objects in his picture in relationship to one another and to the background of his paper. However, as we have seen, he still finds difficulty in recognising the shapes and spaces of words, letters and numbers. This stage of spatial concepts is more usually developed about the age of six. In the same way he has very little concept of time. His reply to the question, how old is someone, may be anything from two to a hundred, although he usually knows his own age because he has been told it many times in relation to his birthday, or to the time when he will come to school. He can reckon time in relation to the day's routine. He knows that dinner happens at a certain time in relation to other happenings, for instance after story time, but abstract names of time, or symbols of time, have very little meaning for him. He is beginning to be able to follow the sequence of events of a story, but if he is asked to repeat that story he is still likely to muddle up the events of that story in time sequence.

The five-year-old, then, is a delightful, happy, co-operative little person. He has come a very long way from the stage of the newborn baby, but at the same time one must always remember that in moments of stress, at times of emotional disturbance, which are bound to happen to the happiest of children, he may revert to patterns of behaviour of a much earlier stage. We must now look at these different stages and patterns of development to see how the transition from the newborn baby to the five-year-old has come about and to see how we can best give him the help, encouragement, and stimuli that he needs, so that he can fulfil each stage successfully.

CHAPTER 2

The first year of life. Patterns of growth. Importance of mother–child relationship. Satisfaction of needs.

As WE have seen, the newborn baby is equipped with all that is necessary to satisfy his needs at this early stage in his life. His needs at this stage are comparatively simple, but as he grows and develops so his needs become greater and of greater complexity. In order to meet these new needs as they arise the child grows and changes. He grows in his capacity to make new adjustments to new situations. This growth proceeds in an orderly fashion and gradually the child functions at a higher level of performance, both physiologically and mentally. As he matures in this way he becomes more capable of dealing with a new situation and of gaining profit from that experience. This progress is gradual and each stage develops from the stage before and leads on to the next one. As Friedrich Froebel wrote, " The vigorous and complete development and cultivation of each successive stage depends on the vigorous, complete and characteristic development of each and all preceding stages of life."*

The greatest and fastest growth is not necessarily the best one, as each child must develop in his own unique pattern. There is a point of " readiness " in each child, at which he can meet with a new experience and deal with it successfully. For example, at a later stage, we have the concept of " reading readiness ", the point at which the child is ready to read. This readiness is evolved from

*Friedrich Froebel, *The Education of Man*, D. Appleton (1887).

the inner maturation of the child, which is a natural growth process, and the stimulus from the outside environment. However, the adjustment to the new situation is not achieved without some difficulty, and sometimes, in the first instance, failures, and therefore the child needs the help of the adults around him in dealing with all new experiences.

The most important adult in the baby's life is the mother or mother-substitute. He is psychologically involved with her and from her he gains his first contacts with the outside world. He has to adjust to the outside world in all the aspects of his development, so she helps him to develop physically by satisfying his needs as they arise. She helps him to develop emotionally and socially by giving him the affection and love to which he will in time respond, and she helps him to develop intellectually by providing for him many stimulating and varied stimuli and experiences. It is essential that the child develops adequately in all these aspects of his development, although he may be more advanced in one aspect than another, but each aspect interacts with the others to give full all-round development, and deprivation in one may mean deprivation in all the others. Thus it has been shown that a child starved of affection will not gain the maximum profit from the food he eats, and moreover will feel insecure and so afraid to make efforts at new physical movements, and this in turn will retard his intellectual development, as he is not having the new experiences necessary for this development.

During the first period of his life the child lives in a rhythmic pattern of sleeping and waking, eating and eliminating, and is making the necessary adjustments to meet the demands of the world outside his mother's womb. As these adjustments stabilise, he becomes more ready for further advances, and in his physical movements he develops usually in a regular pattern. In the first few weeks he will wave his arms about in a circular motion and then these movements become more varied and affected by the position of his head and eyes and may even be controlled by them. He will follow the movement of an object dangled before him with a big movement which takes in the head, the shoulders and the arms. When he is held up he will stretch out his legs, one after the other, almost like a walking movement, and he enjoys sitting up supported by a pillow, and holding up his head. The next step in his development is when he can sit up alone. If an object is put in front of him, he has now so much eye–hand control that he can grasp it and even pass it from one hand to another. This means that he is beginning to gain a sensory impression of space which will help him to direct his movements more adequately. By this time also, at about seven months old, but it must be remembered that any time assessment must be relative to the general developmental pattern of each baby, he can pull himself up and stand, sustaining his whole weight as long as he holds on to something. He has not yet achieved the necessary balance to stand alone. However, he has achieved so much balance that when sitting he can turn to one side or the other, and lean forward and then sit erect again. He can also move from lying down to sitting, and sitting to lying down without help.

He takes a great step forward when he can actually stand by himself without support and begin to walk on his own. This usually happens at about eighteen months and from this point he becomes much more independent of adult help and can begin to experiment more and more in his movements. At this time also he shows a marked development in finer, more delicate movements. He is beginning to move from general mass movements to more specific ones and can now put a ball in a box and place a brick on top of another quite accurately. He can hold a pencil in an overhand grasp and scribble on paper with it. He is now beginning to find new ways of using hands, fingers, legs and feet.

In the same way as in the development of motor characteristics, the baby's social and emotional development proceeds in a regular and orderly pattern. In the earliest weeks, when a face appears before him, he will look at it with a fixed gaze. Occasionally his face may brighten but usually he just looks briefly. He seems to be soothed and calmed when he is picked up and may feel dimly a sense of security. From his reactions it seems to appear that he may differentiate between the way in which he is handled by a calm and secure person or by a worried and nervous one. As he gets older he appears to recognise the touch and voice of his mother, and by about four months old is able to give her a smile when she comes to him. He also appears to become sober when a stranger makes overtures to him. As he is now capable of sitting up he seems to show pleasure at his new view of the world by the brightening of his face.

When he is about seven months old he becomes very involved with his play. He will play for a comparatively long time with one plaything, trying out experiments with it, and he is so absorbed that he pays little attention to the people around him. He appears to be for a time quite self-contained and needs no one. This independent play is most important for his social development. At the same time, when he is not so involved in his play, he looks for interest and attention from the adults around him and takes active measures to get it. He welcomes attention from strangers as well as from those he knows unless they do anything to disturb him.

During the next five months he comes to accept and be part of the routine of the home. He has become a full member of the family group, sleeping all night and taking his food in the same patterns of time as the rest of the family. At the same time he is becoming an individual in his own right. He will do things to attract attention and if the adults laugh at something he does he will repeat it over and over again. He is just at the beginning of recognising himself as someone separate and apart ; he is beginning to realise his own identity. He is also beginning to be aware that strangers are different and he may be cautious about responding to their advances.

He is now showing definite emotional responses of anger, fear and affection and he appears to be aware of the emotions of other people and will react accordingly in the appropriate way. He is beginning to be able to adjust his reactions to other people's behaviour.

The development of language is all-important to the child. Through language he can communicate with other people; he can define to them his needs so that they can be satisfied and he can express his pleasure and contentment when they are satisfied. He can also express clearly his affection for other people and receive in return affection from them. Language is vitally important for his intellectual development as his progress in naming objects and events will help him to clarify his world to himself.

There has been a great deal of research carried out in relation to the development of language in infancy and it has been found, as in all other aspects of development, that progress in language follows a well-defined pattern. There is no doubt that the child understands what other people say to him long before he can use articulate speech himself. But his understanding is more in the nature of understanding of a whole situation which is accompanied by speech rather than of the words themselves. Thus the baby will understand the gestures, facial expression and intonations of the voice as well as the speech, which make up the whole occurrence. The comprehension of actual words comes later.

In the first few weeks of his life the baby shows by his reactions that he is aware of sounds and this is important because it means that when he has reached the right moment in his maturation he will be ready to listen to sounds and later to comprehend them. His chief method of articulation at this stage is crying, and this crying will vary in its strength from time to time, and from one child to another. The only other sounds he makes are small noises in his throat which will be just the beginnings of the babbling of a later stage. These early manifestations show that he is already equipped for speech, but he has to gain, through maturation and practice, more control over his speech organs.

At about four months he has extended his range of noises considerably. He will coo and chuckle, gurgle and laugh. He also shows greater hearing capacity when he turns his head at familiar sounds and he seems to listen in particular to the human voice. Three months later he has made tremendous steps forward in vocalising. He begins to use both consonants and vowels. The fact that he has by this time been given some more solid foods helps him to gain more control over his lips and tongue, and this control makes speech easier for him. The use of single consonants will lead him on to the double consonants, which means that he will soon be saying " ma-ma " and " da-da ". He is also using these vocalisations to make approaches to people and so is developing socially.

At ten months he shows even greater facility in using his tongue and lips. He has one or two sounds that seem like words which he utters clearly and he is beginning to link other methods of expression to the sounds he makes. He will use facial expressions and gestures to accompany his vocalisation and so make his meaning more clear. Moreover, he will imitate the expression on other people's faces and make the same gestures that they do. His comprehension of speech is also developing fast. He will react to the sound of his own name and recognises " no ". He is not yet quite ready to understand the real meaning of other words.

By about a year old he is beginning to take a real part in social interchange. He will listen eagerly to words spoken to him and will try to imitate them. He will repeat the sound of words either to himself, to " practise " them, or repeat them to the adult in imitation. This does not mean that he necessarily understands the words he says, but he is also beginning to show that he can relate actions to words. For example, if an adult says " Give it to me ", he will hand over the object he is playing with. He has now reached the stage of saying " ma-ma " and during the next six months he will add real words to the sounds he makes. The real comprehension of words by the child means that he must be able to pronounce them and that he must be able to relate them to a situation in which he is involved, and then he must be able to use and understand them in a variety of situations.

This is a very brief sketch of the different stages of development through which a child passes in the first year of his life. However, it cannot be stressed too strongly that there are infinite variations in the times at which different babies reach the different stages in their patterns of development. It is the development from stage to stage that is important, not the chronological age at which any given baby reaches any given stage.

Although the baby's natural development and maturation are going on all the time so that he is physiologically ready at different times to meet the demands of new situations, he needs the help of adults to satisfy his needs in the new situation. He cannot do this satisfactorily on his own. The main factor for successful development and satisfaction of needs in this first year of life is a stable mother–child relationship. When the child has lost his own mother he can establish a satisfactory relationship with a mother-substitute, if this relationship is continuous and consistent. It has been found, however, that where the relationship shifts from one adult to another, as may be the case in many Children's Homes, the children are usually retarded in their development. Although they may be well looked after physically, they do not gain the full benefit from the care that is given them. This is particularly true in the social, emotional and intellectual sides of their development. As well as with the constant care of his mother, the child, particularly as he grows older, will develop most favourably in the environment of a happy family life. He will find great pleasure and stimulus in the relationship with his father and with other children in the family, and this will help to prepare him for successful social contacts outside the family.

In order to meet the child's growing needs the parents must be aware of those needs, aware of the stage when the child has reached a " readiness " point for further development. To promote his physical development, they must provide him with the right opportunities at the right time. In the early period he must be given the opportunities to move his limbs freely ; to wave his arms and legs and so gradually develop in strength and control. When he is ready to sit up, he must be well propped up and given encouragement to attempt to sit erect on his own. He will soon feel the pleasure expressed by his mother in those attempts and so will persevere until he is successful. It is the constant encouragement and praise from his mother and family that will help the child in all his learning and provide him with the stimulus to further effort. Although he cannot yet understand the words of praise, he will sense the feelings of satisfaction on his mother's part. This will in turn give him pleasure, and what is pleasurable he is likely to repeat. When his efforts are ignored, or when displeasure is shown by the adults, he is unlikely to attempt that exercise again.

If the child is to take his proper place in society he has to learn to get from place to place on his own. At first he will creep or crawl to the place he wants to reach, but gradually at the right moment he is ready to pull himself up and stand and then when he has achieved enough balance he will walk. But he will not do this entirely on his own. Again he will depend on his mother's help. She will put him down on the floor and encourage him to move towards her. She will give him the right facilities so that he can pull himself up by the sides of his cot or playpen or a conveniently placed chair. She will show him that she is ready to catch him if there is any chance of his falling when he begins to walk. She will supply him with the feeling of confidence that he will succeed and as far as possible she will ensure that he does have success in his attempts at new learning. If he has a failure, as he inevitably will at times, she will be there to comfort him and encourage him to try again if he is ready for that new piece of learning. She will refrain from urging him on to new attempts for which he is not yet maturationally ready. It is as bad to urge him on to new developments before he has reached that readiness point as it is to hold him back, when he has reached that point. It is important that the baby should never feel that she is afraid he might hurt himself in his efforts, as this may hold him back from making those efforts. By her encouragement and by showing her confidence in his ability she will help him to take each new stage naturally and easily.

As he develops through the months of his infancy there comes the time when his need is for more solid and more varied food, and so his mother has to wean him. This inevitably presents difficulty to him. He has to get accustomed to taking all his nourishment from a spoon or a cup and to accept a variety of flavours. As his sense of taste has now become very acute, he may dislike some flavours and he has to be coaxed to take them. Also the lack of physical contact with his mother when feeding may give him a feeling of loss and deprivation, which will cause him distress and make him " difficult ". This means that the situation is not only one of learning physically, but emotionally also. It is one of the early experiences in beginning to become more independent of his mother, and, although he needs this independence, it is at the same time much easier for him to remain dependent. The awareness on the parents' part of the baby's difficulty, accompanied by constant encouragement and affection, will carry him through to success, and because of this happy success he will meet new demands made on him more easily.

The big mass movements of the child, as we have seen, gradually become more specific and he needs to learn a greater control of the finer muscle movements. For this purpose he must be given objects to watch so that he gradually develops a facility in following those objects with his eyes and in reaching out for them, so that he develops greater hand–eye co-operation. He must be given things to grasp that are small enough for him to handle and to pass from one hand to another, and small building bricks that he can bang together or can build one on top of the other when he has the ability to do so. He must be afforded continual opportunities to attempt different kinds of handling, picking up, banging and throwing, and experiencing the feel of different textures. All these opportunities will not only help him with control and co-ordination of his muscles in movement, but will help him to form, at a later stage, concepts of the world about him. He will learn concepts of space from reaching out, and from succeeding in grasping an object which he sees. He will learn concepts of size from handling different objects, and he will learn concepts of sensory discrimination by the feel of different textures, such as rough and smooth, hard and soft. Without these early experiences he will have greater difficulty, later, in forming those concepts, and understanding the world.

In the baby's social and emotional development the mother also has a great part to play. Because of his close relationship with her, he will form his patterns of behaviour on the way she feels and behaves. It is well known that in many cases the nervous, worried mother will have a more difficult nervous baby, whereas the more placid mother tends to have a more placid baby. As he grows slightly older he will be affected by the sound of his mother's voice and will react to the way in which she speaks to him, and later on still he will come to sense the emotional attitudes of the other members of his family. He will be soothed and interested by pleasant-sounding conversation and worried by loud voices quarrelling before he can understand language.

As his mother attends to him and satisfies his needs, he will come to associate feelings of pleasure and contentment with her presence, and as she actually expresses her feelings of love and affection for him, he in turn will develop feelings of love and affection towards her, and later in the same way towards other members of the family. A baby who is not loved, and who is not shown love, will not be able to love anyone himself. He will be disinterested in other people and so will never make the right kind of adjustment to society. As he develops in a loving and secure environment, he will begin to express his feelings of affection and pleasure by making contented, happy noises, by smiling at his mother, and by patting and stroking her face. He will also, however, begin to show actively his feelings of aggression and frustration. These latter demonstrations may be distressing at times, but they also are a sign that he is progressing in his emotional development. His emotional feelings are now becoming more specific and differentiated from one another and he is beginning to show reactions to situations more like those of adults. It is the way in which the adults, particularly his mother, react to these demonstrations of feeling that will help him gradually to subdue the violence and length of these demonstrations. If he is helped over them by comforting him, and by distracting his attention, these outbursts of anger will be of short duration and become less frequent. If on the other hand he feels the adult's disapproval, anger or distress, they are likely to intensify and occur more often. He must, however, be allowed to express his emotions before he can learn to control them. At this early stage he cannot manage to control them by himself, and therefore his mother must do it for him. Although the final aim in this aspect of his development is self-control, he will only learn to achieve this through, in the early stages, being controlled by others.

Socially too, all the child's first learning comes through his mother. His relationship with her will set the pattern of his relationships with others. If he has confidence in her and feels secure when he is with her, he is more likely to welcome contacts with other people. If she shows pleasure when he reacts to her happily, he will seek that feeling of pleasure in relationship with other people. He will smile at people who smile at him and talk to him. However, as he develops, he begins to differentiate between personalities and may cease to make overtures to strangers or respond to them. He may withdraw himself and seek refuge with his mother. It is no use trying to force a child into relationships with strangers. This stage of cautious reaction is again an important growing point in the development of independence. He is just now at the beginning of choosing the people with whom he wishes to have relationships. It is important, however, that he should have the opportunities of meeting with different people so that he can test out his reactions to them, and his mother's reactions to different personalities will inevitably have an effect on his own reactions. He is very quick to sense her feelings towards other people as well as to himself. He will usually make good relationships with older children, but on the whole he shows little interest in other babies. He is too involved with his own growing up to be interested in someone involved in the same process. In order to develop socially then, he must be encouraged in any kind of behaviour that will help him towards independence, and once he has established a firm and stable relationship with his mother and his family, be given opportunities to meet other people.

In the development of language, as in all other aspects, the child needs the help of adults. In every learning situation, as we have seen, he needs praise and encouragement in the meeting of a new situation. He will learn language in the same way, but, perhaps more than in any other aspect of learning he will learn through imitation. Therefore he must be given endless opportunities to imitate. He will learn in the first place, very gradually, that the noises he makes bring him the satisfaction of his needs ; that is, the satisfaction of his hunger, the removal of discomfort, and the satisfaction of being nursed and cuddled. His mother, by her attention to those needs, will show him, as he will gradually understand, that she comprehends what he is trying to gain by his cries.

When he " plays " with sounds, his mother, by imitating them back to him, will give him pleasure, and he will repeat them again and again in order to get the same reaction from her. By her talking to him while she is attending to his wants and while she is playing with him, he will slowly begin to form patterns of sound in his memory which one day he will reproduce. The child must be talked to as much as possible in the early months, in normal language, so that he will have a wide range of sounds to differentiate when he comes to that stage. It is important that when he has reached the right stage his mother should name articles to him as he uses them, so that he will gradually begin to separate specific sounds and relate them to specific things and experiences. His understanding of words will develop from the general to the particular, so that the word " milk ", at first, may mean any kind of food, and " Daddy ", any kind of man. It is only later that he will come to recognise more specific names. It is important, therefore, not to give him too many names at first, but to let his learning be gradual. He will often be able to memorise sounds and words if they are given to him rhythmically, so he has great delight in jingles and nursery rhymes, from an early period. He will enjoy accompanying a jingle with actions, as for instance, in " Pat-a-cake, pat-a-cake ", and these experiences will help him still further to enjoy and practise language. It has been shown that without the help of an understanding mother a baby will be seriously retarded in his language progress and this, in turn, will affect all the other aspects of his development.

By the end of the first year, then, the baby has made great progress. He can now sit, and can stand with support, though he usually cannot yet walk alone. He can use syllables and understand some directions from adults. He can recognise different objects so that he selects the ones he wants to play with, though his choice is often still haphazard. He will recognise his mother and other familiar faces. He has made his first big steps towards independence and he is beginning to emerge as an individual personality in his own right. He is no longer just " the baby " ; he is a character and one of the family.

CHAPTER 3

*From one to three years old. A widening
world and re-orientation. Walking and
talking, toilet training and feeding. New
baby in the family.*

BY THE age of about twelve months the child is beginning to orientate
himself in time to the new rhythms of his own life. By the separation
from the mother through the weaning process he is at the very
beginning of the development of his independence as an individual.
This is further developed by his efforts at standing and walking.
By this new orientation in space as well as in time a whole new
world is opened up to him, therefore this learning to walk is of
vital importance to his all-round development. As in all developmental stages there are great individual differences in the ages at
which the child learns to walk and the mother must be ready to
recognise the signs that show that the child has reached the optimum
moment to attempt this new skill. If this optimum moment is
missed the child may be retarded and the learning process may be
slower. So when the child, after developing the power to pull
himself to his feet, then tries to balance by himself and then takes
steps, the mother's encouragement and help are all-important.
Her pride and pleasure communicate themselves to him and give
him the necessary feelings of success which promote further learning.
When he falls and hurts himself (since some failures are inevitable),
he has first to be comforted and then encouraged to try again.
Never should he be discouraged from trying in case he should

hurt himself, but at the same time, never should he be urged on beyond his own powers of performance.

This independent movement alters the whole view of the world to the baby. Where before the world revolved around his high chair, or cot or pram, now he adventures out into a new world. His sense of spatial relationships alters. The world now becomes a very big space through which he crawls or staggers slowly. His spatial percepts are still not those of the adult world because he is a very small baby in a very large world, but he is beginning to develop sensory comparisons of spatial relationships far more than he was able to do. He finds that some things are big or little, or wide or narrow, although he cannot yet put these percepts into language. He has, by learning to walk, vastly increased the number of first-hand experiences. He finds out for himself that some things are hard and some are soft; that some things move and some stay still; that some things hurt if you bump into them and others do not. He enjoys feeling, stroking and hitting, and because his mouth is most sensitive and therefore gives him most pleasure, everything goes into it. Although there might be danger if everything goes into his mouth yet this oral experimenting plays an important part in his learning.

With the widening of his experience through his independent moving there comes a widening and enrichment of his relationships with other personalities in his environment. Where before people came to him if they wanted to and he had no control over their movements, now he can go after them or away from them. He develops a game of his own of running away in order to be caught and picked up, particularly by his father, and the pleasure of his father is transferred to him so that again he feels success in his achievement. At the same time, because he can now move about fairly freely, he may do things which are not approved of. He may interfere with the occupations of the older children who will be cross with him. In the same way his mother may show her irritation and annoyance with him when he touches things that are dangerous or when he gets dirty. Before he can understand what she is saying he will sense her disapproval from the tone of her voice and will be distressed by it. Through these experiences, although he may be distressed at the time, he is gradually learning the social conventions and the cultural patterns of his society. They are a necessary part of his development.

He now begins to show more differentiation in his reactions to other personalities. He shows more pleasure in one person's company than another's ; but his mother always still comes first. She is the one stable unchanging personality in his environment, but even with her he is beginning to experiment. He is beginning to test her reactions to his behaviour. He will do what she tells him not to do in order to see how she will behave towards him. The consistency of his mother's behaviour in holding to what she has said will give him a feeling of security. He will know what to expect from her, and therefore will gradually build up acceptable patterns of social behaviour. It is essential in order to reach this stage that he should go through this period of experimenting, of trial and error, and of failure and success.

In this difficult period of the beginnings of independent living the child is usually helped by the fact that he is beginning to learn to speak and to understand speech. If he has made a successful experimenting with sounds in his first year he will develop very quickly in understanding and speaking real language. Sometimes, however, if a baby becomes very involved in learning to walk, he seems to slow up for a time in his language development. As with the earlier stages, the mother's teaching of language to the child is all-important. Because of his relationship with her and her praise and encouragement, he will learn quickly, but he needs to be encouraged to speak and to ask for things. Where a child is over-protected and the mother foresees all his wants and supplies them before he can ask, the baby does not feel the need for speech and may be retarded. In the same way children who are brought up in institutions, where they do not have the consistent attention and help of one adult, may also be retarded in their speech. Children who in later life have difficulty with speech or with learning to read and write are often those who, in the early stage of language learning, were either over-protected or neglected. As in all aspects of development, there are also great differences in the times at which children begin to speak. Sometimes a child who appears to be slow in attempting to speak may miss out vocally the early baby stages of speech and will suddenly speak correctly in sentences with the right constructions. He has been learning internally. The child usually understands more than he speaks, but at the same time, because he is intensively imitative at this stage and memorises very easily, he gives the appearance of understanding more than he actually does. It is only when he has had words used in all different kinds of contexts and experiences that he comes to be more specific in his use of them. He will use words for communication, to express his needs, but also for aesthetic pleasure. He enjoys using words and will repeat a word that catches his fancy, over and over again. It is the very beginning of his appreciation of literature.

As he becomes more adept in his use of language, at between two and three years old, he will begin to accompany his actions with words. He will talk in a monologue, especially if someone he knows is near, describing to himself what he is doing. This speech is always accompanied by action. He is clarifying to himself not only what he is doing but also his understanding of language ; the two go together. In this way he is beginning to form mental concepts built on the sensory percepts which he has acquired through all the first hand experiences he has had in his play. It is up to the mother to help him in this clarification of language and experience by giving him exact and precise words to fit the situation. One would deprecate the use of " baby " words and phrases as the child has only to learn a different word for that object later, and he will not be able to relate word and object when adults discuss the same object amongst themselves. It is as easy for him to learn the right word as a baby equivalent.

This is the time when the child takes great pleasure in picture-books. Pictures should be clear and natural, depicting objects that are within the child's experience so that he begins to recognise pictorial and two-dimensional representations of objects that he knows in a three-dimensional sphere. The naming of these pictorial objects by the mother will gradually bring to recognition within the child's mind the relationship between these representations and the real objects. This is the beginning of the recognition of symbolic representation which he will have to acquire in his later learning of reading, writing and arithmetic. One would stress, at this point, however, the necessity of remembering that because of the child's lack of ability to use his eyes in focusing on small objects and his lack of appreciation of spatial relationship, it is not easy for him to distinguish small pictures from one another. These are two skills which will not develop properly until much later and like all stages of learning must not be forced. To try to teach a child a skill before he is ready for it will only retard his ultimate development in that skill and may set up an emotional bias against that learning.

By three years old the child has made tremendous steps forward in his intellectual development. By learning to move about independently he has increased his perceptual experiences. Now he can go to places and find out for himself. He is endowed with a natural inquisitiveness and curiosity which stand him in good stead in his learning. Sometimes the adults may deplore the fact that the child is so inquisitive, but without it he would learn very little. It is the self-initiated finding out of the child which is most beneficial to his easy natural mental development.

Besides acquiring the actual ability to get around by walking, the child is developing physically in other ways. At first his walk has been a staggering, stumbling, top-heavy effort, needing outstretched arms to achieve balance, but as he practises the new skill he acquires greater control over the co-ordination of muscles. A child of three does not usually walk in a steady, regular manner; he walks a little, runs a little, sits down or squats. He still helps his balance by having his feet apart and his knees slightly bent. When he turns a corner he still goes round in a curve; he cannot yet achieve a sharp-angled turn. He will, as he runs, stretch out his arms to show himself the direction in which he is travelling and the object he wants to reach. He can move rhythmically to music if the rhythm is slow enough for him. Occasionally he will keep time to an adult's rhythm, but more often he creates his own rhythmic patterns within those of the adult.

As a very young baby he has been able to support his whole weight by clinging with his hands and now even at three he enjoys climbing as much as walking. Small children can be seen in any Nursery School climbing with confidence to the top of the jungle gym or swinging on parallel bars with their whole weight dependent on their arms. A young two-year-old will " squat " for long periods absorbed in play, in a position which an adult would find very tiring, but he would rather hold that position than sit on a chair or even on the floor. It is more comfortable for the proportions of his limbs and gives him more ease of movement. A child of this age can throw a ball, more or less in the right direction, but because he still finds it easier to hold on than to let go, he often holds the ball too long, so that the impetus is lost, or he releases it too early with the same result. He still finds difficulty in timing his muscle control. He has not yet acquired full binocular vision and his eyes do not yet work together in a fully mature way, so he cannot follow a ball thrown to him, with his eyes, so that he catches successfully. He will, if shown how, put his hands together, but if by chance he does catch the ball, it is usually between wrist and elbow, not between his hands.

He has usually achieved, by the age of three, enough hand–eye co-ordination to hit a wooden peg through a hole with a hammer, but finds difficulty in hammering a much smaller nail into a piece of wood. He will fill a pail with sand, but finds difficulty in the quick turning out movement, necessary to make a sand pie. He can us a large paint brush, but his grasp is more often than not an overhand one and the movement of the brush is from the shoulder and elbow and not from the wrist. Most of his movements are still whole body movements. He can now do a certain amount of his own dressing. He can undo easy buttons but finds buttoning more difficult. He can with a great effort pull up his own pants, but still needs help in adjusting the clothes under them. He can wash the palms of his hands but still finds the backs difficult.

In his social development the child is still very egocentric. He is the centre of his world in his own mind. What he does, he thinks is right, and what he says is right, and he is distressed when his mother shows disapproval of him, though this at times is necessary. To his way of thinking he has the first right to any toy, the first right to any food. It is quite wrong to expect any child of this age to be unselfish, though we may encourage him in elementary ways to begin to think of others. One of the first words he learns and uses constantly is " mine ". Everything is " mine " from his mother downwards. He would never consider sharing his toys and sweets, although he might do so on odd occasions in order to win his mother's approval. When he gives something to another child and his mother says " good boy ", he will repeat the action, not because he is unselfish, but in order to win praise for himself. This is, however, not an intellectually thought out action. As with the higher animals, he discovers through trial and error that giving something away brings the reward of praise, just as withholding that object brings disapproval and perhaps scolding. Therefore he performs the action that brings reward. It is this approval of adults in the early stages that will bring him, when he is ready, to the stage of true altruism.

The child has a rather different relationship with his father from that with his mother. He sees much less of him and, at any rate at first, is less emotionally involved with him. He is the strong personality of the family and as he admires and loves the child, so the child comes to love and admire him. Because he is not so involved in the training of the child and therefore does not have to show as much disapproval at times as the mother does, the child does not have as many feelings of guilt about him at this stage and so is nearly always good and well-behaved with him. He does not identify himself with the father yet, nearly as much as he identifies himself with his mother. This is a later stage of his development. At this time, too, he is beginning to make relationships with the other children in the family. They usually show pride and affection for him, although on the part of the next youngest there may be some jealousy. The young child is only too anxious for all the attention he can get from familiar personalities and he will gradually differentiate between the children, liking the attention of one more than the others. It is difficult to understand sometimes why he favours one child above another, but most families know that this does happen even in the early months. This widening of the child's interactions with persons of different ages within the small community of the family is most important for the later development of social relationships in a wider community like the classroom. If a child is confident and secure in a small group, he is less likely to be frightened when he goes to school or when he later goes into an adult working world. A child who has not been successful in his early relationships will have much greater difficulty in finding his place in the world and may remain shy and withdrawn all his life. If the baby is an only child, it is wise for the mother, when he is getting on for three years old, to arrange that he meets with other children of his own age, or slightly older, preferably within the safety of his own home, or at any rate in his mother's presence. He may play with them only for very short intervals, but he will play alongside them and so get used to having other children around. Children under three usually prefer to play alone, but they show interest in what other children are doing and make occasional contacts with them, although quite often these first contacts may be aggressive ones. The small two-year-old may hit another child if that child has a toy that he wants, or if he has not met another child before, he may hit him simply in order to experiment, to see what happens. No one is more surprised than he when the other child cries or hits him back. These experimental aggressive overtures are frequently the beginnings of friendliness and real social relationships.

In his emotional development the child is very much at the mercy of his own intensely strong feelings. He has no control over them and he must express them immediately, actively and physically.

If he is angry he throws a temper tantrum. He throws himself on the floor, screams loudly, thrashes arms and legs about, and if an adult tries to pick him up he goes rigid and stiff and refuses to relax. No amount of specific comforting will quieten him but he can be distracted and soothed by calling his attention to something else. It is no use scolding or punishing the child for behaving in this way. He does not know consciously what he is doing and if too much disapproval is shown he will develop unconscious but intense feelings of guilt at having hurt his mother, and this will make him frightened, easily disturbed, and therefore more quickly aggressive. He expresses his love as violently as his anger. His loving embrace of his mother or someone he likes can nearly throttle them. There are no half measures about the expression of emotions on the part of a two-year-old.

One very difficult period which the child has to go through between the ages of one and three is that of toilet training. All mothers are anxious that their babies should be " clean ", and take great pride in them if they achieve this early. But the time when babies are ready to accept this training differs greatly from one baby to another. If under pressure a baby is trained successfully very early he may later regress to the earlier stage and the mother is faced with lack of control of both bladder and bowel. This in turn may mean that he will then take even longer to achieve success because of his failure. Pressure may mean that too much is made of the training. The child is extravagantly praised when he is successful and the mother is inordinately disappointed when he fails. The transition from baby to adult performance in this aspect of his development is very difficult and may with some babies take a long time. It takes endless patience, plenty of encouragement, and no fuss if possible about failures. The conquering of this difficult stage is a very big step forward for the child, especially when he can manage wholly by himself. He will gain in feelings of confidence and self-reliance, not only in matters connected with the toilet, but in other respects also, and he begins to be no longer a baby but a child. It must be remembered, however, that in moments of anxiety, fear or distress the child may still revert to the earlier patterns of behaviour and have an " accident ", and in this case he needs all the sympathy and reassurance he can get because he has lapsed, not only from his mother's standards for him, but also from his own unconscious ideal of his own competence. He is overwhelmed by his guilty feelings and his confidence in his own powers must be restored again as soon as possible or his fears of failure will cause that very failure.

This stage of emergence from babyhood to childhood, from about one to three years old, is of great importance in giving the child a sense of confidence in his own powers to get about and to meet the world at his own level. He is still dependent on his mother, still very egocentric and still prefers to play alone, although he is just beginning to make contacts with other children. He still prefers to have adults for company who give him a sense of security and comfort. He still has no control over his emotions, and expresses them physically and violently.

Although he can use language, it is used to express his own immediate needs or to try to explain to himself what he is doing. He cannot express himself logically nor deal with abstract ideas. He has as yet no real sense of time or spatial relationships, and although he may use words relating to time concepts and to space concepts, he has as yet no real understanding of them. We must at this stage be very much aware of overestimating the child's understanding of language. He has developed so much in so short a time that it is very easy to expect too much from him. At the same time we must not underestimate the importance of the fact that now that the child can use language he is released from some of the tensions which result from his frustration at not being able to make the adults understand what he wants at any given time.

By the time the child is three he will be able to feed himself fairly adequately with a spoon and drink from a cup without spilling. He will be developing definite likes and dislikes over his food and may express these forcibly. There may be times when he refuses to eat, either one article of food, or if he is not feeling well, all his food. When he finds that his mother makes a fuss of him in order to get him to eat, he may resort to being difficult over food at other times in order to get that extra attention. At the same time one must remember that if the child is emotionally upset he will not assimilate his food properly even if he is forced to take it, and therefore such pressure is a wasted effort. This pressure also may create for him a fear and dislike of the food which caused it. He can often be coaxed and encouraged, without fussing, to eat a little of the food, particularly if his attention is distracted to something else. If such encouragement fails, then ignoring the incident, or simply removing the plate, will often mean success on the next occasion.

Usually a child can be trusted to do what is best for his own development unless he has been conditioned by adults to be difficult about his food. A child is a great imitator and he will quickly follow the example of adults he loves and admires. If the mother does not like certain articles of food, even although she does not express her dislike openly the child will sense it and follow her lead. One group of children in a Nursery class were very difficult about drinking their hot milk in the winter time and it was discovered that the teacher of that class had a marked dislike of hot milk. Although she never expressed her dislike openly, the children had sensed it and reacted accordingly. When the class assistant was left in charge of the milk period the children's attitude changed and there was no more trouble. A child may be conditioned very easily by the way in which things are said to him. For instance, if he is told, " Finish up your first course and you will have some nice pudding ", the inference to the child is not only that pudding is nice, but also that the first course is not nice. Many children are conditioned to being difficult over taking medicine because the mother promises them a reward for taking it, thereby implying that it is unpleasant. If something is really unpleasant (and that to a child usually means something bitter), then the child should be warned that he may not like it and should be given something sweet after it. It is most important that the adult should never lie to the child, because if his trust and confidence is once betrayed he is lost and bewildered and he may come to distrust everyone. If one has to give a child physical pain, as, for instance, in dressing a wound, then he should be told that it will hurt. In the same way, if the mother has to leave the child for a time he should be told about it beforehand. The shock of finding suddenly that his mother is not there can be very damaging to his development, and the younger the child, the greater the damage will be. The greatest fear of the child under five is that of desertion by his mother, and because the child under three has no time sense and so little understanding of language, it is almost impossible to make him understand and realise that his mother is coming back. He can stand being out of her presence for a short period if he knows that she is within call, but sometimes if she is only in the next room, he will have to rush in to make quite sure that she has not gone. This is one of the main reasons why most Nursery Schools today, although legally they may take children from two to five years old, do not accept children under three, except in the most exceptional cases.

One of the greatest difficulties a child of this age (or indeed of any age, but it is more acute under three) has, is that of the mother " deserting " him in order to go into hospital to have another baby. However carefully the child is warned about it beforehand, however carefully he has been prepared, he still suffers a great shock. In the first place there is his desertion by his mother. This means to the child, unconsciously, that it is his fault. He must have done something bad and therefore his mother no longer loves him and has gone away from him. Then when she comes back, she brings with her a new baby who usurps his place in her arms and claims a great deal of her attention. The new baby claims not only her attention but also the interest and admiration of all the other members of the family, and he appears to be left out in the cold. All children, however good the home situation may be, are bound to feel some jealousy of the new member of the family. The problem is exacerbated for the child if the mother has been over-protective to him and has refused to allow him to make relationships with other adults or other members of the family. Different children will show their resentment and jealousy in different ways. One of the most common ways is by reversion to earlier patterns of behaviour, when the child becomes incontinent, refuses to eat, insists on climbing on his mother's lap or follows her round whining for attention. It may show physically in his appearance ; he has dark circles round his eyes and a pale peaky face. He may even attack the baby physically, tip him out of his cot, pinch him or hit him, but yet at the same time he may protest that he loves him, admires him and will talk to him in the way his mother does. He may try to work out his aggression on his toys by ill-treating them, throwing them about or breaking them, or he may attempt to work out his anger on any pets there are in the house. One little girl, for instance, while the new baby was being bathed and occupying most of her mother's attention, used to persist in smacking the dog, who luckily took it all in good part as a game. The most harmful type of behaviour is perhaps that of the child who withdraws from the situation. An example of this is of a bright little girl of three who was happy and independent, could speak well and enjoyed life to the full. After the advent of the baby she refused to have any contact with her mother. She refused to speak at all ; she had disturbed sleep at night ; she had great difficulty with her food ; she lost weight ; she refused to play with anyone or anything or make any kind of contacts. It was eighteen months before she began to act normally again, by which time she had fallen away behind her normal development.

This is of course an extreme case, and most children adjust fairly quickly to the new situation. The mother can help in many ways to ease it for the child. He must be warned well in advance by the mother's talking to him about all the things that they will be able to do with the new baby. She must stress the fact that it will be his baby as well and the importance of his helping her with it. We know that the child will not understand all the implications of what she says, but he will get some ideas to which she can refer later. One family helped the situation when a new baby arrived, by the mother coming in alone on her arrival from hospital to greet the child and by the father bringing in the baby about ten minutes later. This helped the child to accept the newcomer more easily. The mother can also try to get the child to help her with the baby as much as possible. He can help her to push the pram and help her bath the baby by handing her the flannel and towel. In many ways he can help her by fetching and carrying things and so get a feeling of importance. At first the child should never be left alone with the baby in case he should hurt it, either through aggressive feelings or simply because he wants to experiment with it and find out all about it. If he does interfere with the baby, even if he does not actually hurt it, the mother is bound to show her disapproval and the child will be full of guilty feelings which may make him even more aggressive towards the baby. It is very important that a mother should continue to give as much of her time as possible to the older child. It has been found valuable if she can have a special time with him after the baby has been put to bed and out of the way. It may encourage him to accept the situation if she looks at pictures of babies with him or tells him stories about them, at the same time cuddling him on her lap as she does with the baby. The father can often help out too by giving the first child more of his time than he used to do, to try to make up to him for the loss of so much of his mother's attention. He may also be helped by the provision of the right kind of play materials, which will be discussed later.

Quite often mothers think that because they have less time to give to the older child, this is the time to send him to a Nursery School or Class, but if one thinks of it from the child's point of view, one realises how harmful this could be. It will seem to the child like a second desertion by his mother. First she goes away herself and then she sends him away while she stays at home with the new baby in his place. Once again the child is filled with guilty fears. He is convinced that his mother can do no wrong; she is always right. Therefore it must be something very bad that he has done for her to punish him in this way. Unfortunately because the child unconsciously feels like this, he may withdraw into himself completely and appear in the Nursery School to be very good and amenable. He appears to have settled in well, whereas in actual fact he is terrified of drawing attention to himself and only wants to be ignored. It is much better, if the mother is going to send her child to a Nursery School, to wait for two or three months until the child has adjusted to the new home situation before imposing on him another heavy burden of adjustment.

Before the age of three is the time when the child is just beginning to wonder and admire. He is excited by everything new, particularly in the natural world. There is no fear or dislike in the two-year-old for insects, worms or spiders; he is fascinated by them. Out in the country or on the seashore everything holds for him excitement and wonder. If he lives in a town flat, every opportunity should be made to take him out where he can see trees and grass. Even the limited opportunities of a town park are better than nothing. Natural objects can be brought into the home for him to look at and study and the present vogue for indoor plants and window boxes gives him the chance to see growing things and so convey to him some of the mysteries of the life cycle. These experiences cannot start too early for him, and in our modern city life too many young children are deprived of them. If the child has these sensory experiences to satisfy his curiosity, wonder and awe at this early stage, they will develop later into experiences of intellectual appreciation and spiritual understanding.

By the time the child reaches the age of three he is definitely moving out of infancy into childhood. He is beginning to be independent of his mother, although he has continually to return to her for security. He is just beginning to realise other persons in their own right although he is still the centre of his picture. Since the age of two he has trebled his language content and this makes life easier for him in communicating and in expressing his emotions in a rather more socially acceptable way. He is beginning to realise his place in the community as an individual, although he has a long way to go before he comes to a full understanding of this. He is now ready to go on to further development from the ages of three to five.

CHAPTER 4

From three to five. Growing independence.
Facility in speech. Difficulties in
relationships. Emergence of the individual.

IF THE child has gone successfully through the different stages from one to three years old, and has, with his mother's help, conquered the difficulties that beset him on the way, he is ready to go on through the next two years which will bring him to a greater independence of his mother and other adults and into a stage of social relationships with children of his own age, though the fullness of this development will not be reached until he is eight or nine years of age.

Physically at three he is at a transitional stage. Although he can walk and run and even skip, his co-ordination fails him at times and he falls over and he has to start all over again. He still finds climbing an easy exercise and still uses his arms more than his legs to support his weight. He will put one foot up and then bring the other up beside it before going on to the next step or rung. He may miss a step and hang by his arms, and in that case he may be frightened and needs reassurance and encouragement to try again. Without such encouragement he may be too frightened to try again and will go back in his development of muscular control. In running, he still turns corners in a curve, since angles are too difficult for him to take sharply. If he does not take the corner of a wall " wide " he may bump into it. In running he throws his head back in order to keep his balance and so may easily trip over something or even his own feet. In jumping he will jump with two feet together and does not get very far off the ground. If he jumps off a height he still keeps two feet together and prefers the help of an adult hand.

As at two, he still finds finer, more delicate movements, not very easy. He is, however, attempting to use a brush and pencil in an adult way and no longer with the overhand grasp. He is also becoming more adept in washing hands and putting on clothes, though he still needs adult help. With clay, sand and dough he is beginning to use his fingers more instead of his whole hand, and sometimes manages to hold a nail to knock it into a piece of wood.

Between the ages of three to four he usually goes through a rather difficult time emotionally. Where before much behaviour which has not been acceptable to adults has been excused because he was only the baby, now that he is getting around on his own and is becoming a personality in his own right, much more is expected of him in adjusting to adult standards of behaviour. He is expected to know what is good and what is naughty, and to behave accordingly. This often causes him great frustration and feelings of guilt may arise. Although he can behave as is expected of him when the adult is there, when she is not with him he cannot remember her standards of behaviour. This is a natural stage of development. It is literally true of the under four-year-old that " out of sight is out of mind ". His mother will say in exasperation that she cannot take her eyes off him for a minute without his getting into mischief ; this is true because so often to him " mischief " is merely the natural and attractive thing for him to do. He has not nearly reached the stage when he has assimilated and made part of himself adult standards of behaviour. What in adult parlance is messy, or dirty, or destructive, is natural to his primitive impulses, and these strong impulses must be acted upon immediately. When his mother is there, his need for her love and approval will help him to control those impulses, but when she is not there and he is thrown on his own resources he cannot control them or realise the necessity for doing so. Primitive impulses must be satisfied, but they must be satisfied in a socially acceptable way, so that the child does not develop guilty feelings about them. This can be done by the provision of the right materials and equipment either in the home or the Nursery School, and this will be dealt with later. Another way of helping him to accept adult standards is by praise for good behaviour, which makes him feel strong and in control of the situation and which therefore he will repeat. This will have far more effect than any amount of scolding or punishment for lapses from acceptable behaviour.

This is the period also during which most children go through difficulties in relation to the family situation. When he is about three and a half to four and a half he begins to become more aware of himself as a separate personality, particularly if he comes into contact with other children. In becoming aware of himself he becomes aware of other personalities and their different relationships with one another. Before this stage everyone had only a relationship with himself, his mother, his father and his siblings. Now he begins to be aware of, and puzzled by, the relationship between his father and his mother. He begins to sense that there is a particular and unique relationship between them in which he has not any part. He begins by being puzzled and then frightened. Anything he does not understand in human relations tends to frighten him. He needs his mother's support, but feels that she has deserted him for his father, and so there grows in him feelings of jealousy for his father. Like all emotions in the early years, this is very strong and intense and it is made even more difficult and frustrating for him in that he still feels the great love and admiration for his father that he had before this happened. He wants to be like his admired father and therefore at the same time hold the same place in respect of his mother that his father does. He cannot control the situation or his feelings as an adult can, and therefore he tends to try to revert to the safety of his earlier position in the family. He goes back to earlier patterns of behaviour, only this time it is not the natural developmental pattern.

Each action is motivated by the strong feelings of aggression and deprivation. So he refuses to sleep, refuses to eat, is incontinent in bed or during the day. He takes to thumb sucking and cries a lot, and worst of all he will not let his mother out of his sight. One must remember that all the time he is afraid himself of these strong feelings which he cannot control, and is aware of his mother's disappointment and disapproval of him, which increases his feelings of insecurity and deprivation. Therefore, one cannot treat him as a naughty child. He needs help, not punishment. At the same time he must be made aware by his mother that this kind of behaviour is not acceptable. However, she must also show him that she still loves him by giving him a little extra attention. Even more important, at this stage the father can give the child help by giving him as much attention as possible. If he can get him to feel that they are both men together, doing things that women cannot, like carpentry, or doing things to the car, the child will get that feeling of male superiority, which can protect his mother from harm. He can change his role from that of the dependent child to that of the strong protector, and therefore he is still an important member of the family circle. One small four-year-old, sitting on the couch between his father and much older brother, remarked, with great satisfaction, " We three men ".

In the case of a girl child, this stage operates in a rather different way although the results are more or less the same. The little girl, who usually adores her father, comes to be jealous of her mother's position in the father's love. She wants to hold that position herself, and she senses some mystery about the position of father, mother, and baby relationship, which she cannot understand. She becomes antagonistic to her mother, although she still loves her intensely. This brings with it, therefore, as in the case of the boy, feelings of great guilt and loss of security. When the mother sees the child hanging round her father, constantly demanding his attention, she may feel annoyed and perhaps unconsciously a little jealous, which is quite natural. The father must obviously give the attention which the child demands within reasonable limits, but the mother can do more for the child by getting her to help her in doing things for the father. Giving her small, responsible jobs for the father, like fetching things for him, so that in this case it is the women who are looking after the man together. It must be realised by both father and mother that this is a normal stage of development through which all children pass in varying degrees, and that where no fuss is made, and the child is supported and helped by the affection of both parents, it will not last long. If the child does not go through this normal time, normal that is, for the child's own individual pattern of development, which will vary from child to child, he will go through it at a later stage when it will probably be much more severe. The child who can express openly and aggressively that things are not going right with him is much easier to help than the child who becomes very quiet and appears to be good. When the child between three and five is always very quiet, very obedient and never in trouble, he needs a lot of help and understanding. This jealousy stage is made even more acute for the child if it coincides with the arrival of a new baby in the family. We have already discussed this situation, but if the two do come together the child may have a very difficult time. However, children are amazingly resilient, and given love and understanding by their parents will overcome what, to an adult, might appear an insuperable mound of problems.

When the child of three to four is not engaged in these problems he is an engaging and delightful person. He expects everyone to be friends with him and be interested in him, and he is ready to be friends with everyone. He is beginning to take an interest in other children, though rather in an experimental fashion. He is interested and sometimes disturbed if another child cries, and if that crying becomes loud and aggressive, he may cry too. On the other hand, if another child laughs he may join in that laughter, either in imitation or sympathy. This is just the beginnings of real social relations with his contemporaries. Normally at this stage there is not much real playing together of children, although it varies greatly with individuals. He likes to play alongside other children, sometimes showing interest in what they are doing, sometimes passing a remark, but still quite self-sufficient with what he himself is doing. He may show aggression to another child who has a toy which he wants, or who is getting attention from an adult. He still believes that the world is his and it is his right to be the centre of attention. However, this is the time when he should be beginning to meet other children, to become aware of their claims to attention, so that when the right developmental stage is reached he will be ready for companionship and will make a happy adjustment to society.

One must not expect a child of this age even yet to be unselfish or to be aware of the needs of others. Where at two he might give away sweets in order to be praised, and does not realise that once the sweets are gone he cannot have them, now he has the foresight to know this and so will not give them away. He has learned by experience. His mother feels that her former unselfish child has become selfish and is disappointed in him, but the fact that he has become selfish means that he has reached a further stage in his development and is therefore to be welcomed. He has a long way to go before he becomes truly altruistic, but this does not mean that the mother should do nothing to help towards this further stage. Always he should be praised for any signs of unselfish behaviour. Quite often the need in the Nursery School for sharing the favourite toys, or in taking turns on the swing or tricycle, makes him realise for the first time that other people have claims to, and rights in, things which he has considered his own personal possessions. This is a very difficult concept for him to accept, and does at times cause emotional disturbance, but with support and praise and fair dealing he will come to give in to another child. Quite often the praise of the adult is of more value to him than the use of the desired toy. Often to the adult the child's demands seem trivial and we cannot understand what all the fuss is about, but the child identifies himself with the object he is playing with. In giving it up, he is giving up something of himself and as he is going through the stage of becoming independent of his mother, every difficulty looms much larger. Also, because he has not yet had enough experience of time concepts, he cannot realise that he will have another turn later, and so the adult has to have endless patience with his continual repetition of the phrase, " It's my turn now ", or " Is it my turn now ? "

In his intellectual development also he makes great steps forward. He is beginning to use language more fluently and to explore the possibilities of language. He uses it first for communication. He can now tell the adult what he wants, but as his understanding is still limited the adult does not always understand what he means. This is to him a shock. He is still, as I have said, the centre of his world, and it is inconceivable that anyone should misunderstand him. *He* understands what he wants, therefore everyone else *must* understand him. It is interesting to note that when he is trying to communicate with adults, as in the Nursery School situation, other children may understand him better than the adults do and will translate for him. His mother has much less trouble in understanding him than other adults because of her close relationship with him. She seems to operate on the same wavelength. If a child is not understood he becomes furiously frustrated and angry. This is why a child who is retarded in his speech development does appear more emotionally disturbed and difficult than one who has developed well on this side. There seems to be little doubt that mixing with other children does help a child to develop in language because of the need for communication with others who are not interested in him particularly. They are too busy with themselves and their own development. Also he will tend to imitate other children's speech as an interesting form of play. At the same time, because he is still in the egocentric stage, he will expect other children to understand him, just as he does with adults. Also he will not put himself out to try to understand what another child is saying unless it has some real bearing on what he himself is doing or saying, or unless it fits into the pattern of his own scheme. He is not really interested in other children's behaviour as such, only in relation to his own. We as adults, therefore, must endeavour to understand the child's world with him and when he appears to understand us, or express what he wants, we must be wary of accepting what he says at the adult level. He is still performing at his own level which may have totally different concepts from ours. He understands himself in his world, not ours.

The child at this stage has a very good mimicry memory. By the age of four, if given the opportunities, he can repeat a great number of nursery rhymes and jingles. Quite often he can count up to twenty, say his own name and address and age, but this does not mean that he understands what he is saying. If he has a story read to him often enough, he will himself take the book and " read " the story, but if two pages are turned over at once, or the book is upside down, he will still give you the story word for word. He has not yet achieved the skill of relating symbols to reality, to what he says or does, though he can see the relation between the book his mother reads and the story she tells. In number, though he will talk about big and little, these have for him very little meaning in the adult sense of the words. Big is to him what is important in his world, so that when he is, at four, painting or drawing a human figure, much the largest part is the head and face, often taking up at least two-thirds of the figure. The head and face of his mother is one of his first visual experiences, and because that experience has brought with it pleasure and satisfaction, that to him is important and therefore big. A child of this age paints what he knows, not what he sees in the reality world of the adult. In the same way he has as yet no real number concepts. A large number to him may be two or a hundred or a million. They are just pleasant words to him which he enjoys using, particularly if the adult laughs with him when he makes an extraordinary numerical phrase. If you ask a child how old you are, he will say the first number that comes into his head, for example, three or a thousand. We do tend to over-estimate the child's ability in the use of number concepts because he is so fluent, there is no hesitation on his part, and he is so sure of himself.

He has as yet no sense of spatial relationships. In his painting he may paint in the corner of the paper. He may draw the figure of a man and put the eyes alongside the head, not in the face, or the arms alongside and parallel to the body, not attached to it. The face and eyes, body and arms, are all in his mind, part of the same whole body, but the parts do not necessarily bear relation to one another. He simply shows this belongingness by juxtaposition; that is sufficient for his purpose. In the same way with his lack of realisation of space he believes he can " reach the sky ", that an aeroplane can be touched by him. To his mind he can climb anything or go anywhere. If a thing can be seen it can be touched by his all-powerful self. This is why the child so often gets into trouble, because he will climb after or reach up to things beyond his reach, and may fall or break something in the process. This understanding of spatial relationships does not usually come to the child before the age of about six, and we must not expect it of him. However, although the child has not yet reached the age of understanding numerical concepts, spatial relationships, and relationships between symbols and experiences, either in action or speech, we must provide him with the greatest number and variety possible of practical experiences which will lay the foundation of his later understanding. The adult must give the child the words to go with these practical experiences so that when he reaches the right stage in school he will be able to relate these practical experiences both to the spoken and written symbols. But he must go through the physical, sensory, stage before he can come to the abstract stage. The reason why many children, or adults for that matter, dislike arithmetic, is because abstract manipulation of number concepts is forced upon them before they have enough practical experiences. These must come first and may have to be reverted to again and again, in the case of any individual child, before real understanding occurs.

When a child reaches four he seems again to make a great leap forward. He has got over the transitional stage of the three-year-old and suddenly becomes independent and companionable in his own right as a person. Physically he has acquired many skills. He runs faster and with much more confidence. He looks where he is going and can swerve to avoid obstacles, and is beginning to take corners at an angle. He can skip in time to a tune and march with emphasis, keeping a good rhythm. He is very skilful in using a tricycle and can steer it at full speed, and finds great pleasure and satisfaction in his control of his first machine. In throwing a ball he has learnt how to release the ball in time so that he can direct it more accurately. His hand–eye co-ordination is not yet fully developed enough to ensure his catching a ball, but he is beginning to have some success now and again. He is also showing some skill in kicking a large ball, and though he cannot usually direct it yet he manages to make his foot contact the ball and retain his balance while doing it. He climbs stairs one foot after another without bringing his feet together in between and in climbing a jungle gym uses his feet and legs more, and arms less, to support his weight. On parallel bars he can hang upside down by his knees and can with some help turn a somersault over them. In smaller muscular movements he is also gaining more control, and more hand–eye co-ordination. Thus he can fill a pail and turn out a sand pie ; he can pour water from one vessel to another without spilling and can spoon food from a serving dish on to his plate. He can wash his hands and face and comb his hair, fasten his coat-buttons though he still has some difficulty with unbuttoning. He can fasten buckles or sandals which are not too stiff, but tying shoe-laces usually defeats him. In painting he uses a large brush with ease and holds it in an adult manner and can put the paint where he wants it on the paper.

By the end of the period he has enough finger control to cut with scissors, though he still has difficulty in following a cutting line, and he can place the pieces of a jigsaw puzzle together with accuracy. Altogether he has learnt a great many new skills which will help him to become still further independent of adult help so that he will be more ready to take his place in the Infant School. There is, however, one caveat about his readiness for the Infant School. Although his binocular vision has improved and he can focus more easily, he is not yet ready for any fine work of any description. In particular he is not yet usually ready to learn to read. The physical effort for a child first learning to read is very great. He has to focus his eyes on the beginning of a line of print, take in a number of symbols, and then stop before going on to the next batch. Then he has to make a new adjustment from the end of the first line of print to the beginning of the second, making a diagonal line. Quite often he will miss the beginning of the second and go on to the third. Even an adult, when tired, will do this, so one can understand how much more difficult for a child, who has only just learnt this difficult skill of focusing, this can be. It takes intense concentration on his part, which sometimes he cannot sustain, and hence reading may be an unsatisfactory experience for him, especially if the adult expresses disapproval. Many children are now going into the Infant School before the age of five and in many cases are expected to begin to learn to read right away ; this is almost impossible for them, and even when the child is physically mature enough, periods of learning to read should be chosen by the child himself, who knows when he can no longer concentrate enough to be successful. He may be encouraged to read and guided to read, but never pressurized into reading.

Emotionally the child between four and five seems to settle down to a more equable period. Once he has gone through and conquered the intense aggressions and ambivalent behaviour caused by the jealousy of the father, mother relationship, he comes to accept his place in the family. Where there are siblings, he begins to find his place among them too, and the intensity of his emotions may become toned down as he spreads his affections further afield. He comes to feel love and affection for other adults, and in receiving back love and affection from them he may lose a little of the intensity of his love for his mother. She is still the centre of his attention, and when things go wrong she is still the one for whom he cries, but he is not identifying quite so much, with her. Mothers are sometimes unwilling to see their children making other relationships of this kind. They cannot bear the thought of another adult perhaps taking their place in the child's affections, but it is imperative for the child's own good development that he should gradually grow away from his mother, and dependence. The child cannot yet stand on his own feet, and when his mother is not there he needs the help of another adult to make the transition to full independence.

If the mother encourages him to make these other relationships, she will find that she still retains all his love and confidence, but if she stands in the way of such development, he may show antagonism to her. For a child to develop to his fullest potential he must be able to be independent, to cope with his own difficulties, to make his own judgements and to stand on his own feet. Perhaps it is one of the most difficult periods in her relationship with the child when she has to let him go and feels she is losing him. The child, however, at four and five, will only feel safe in his new relationships if he is secure in the knowledge that his mother is always there to go back to. Whatever he does, he is secure in her love, and so can experiment and be naughty with her when he dare not do so with other adults. Sometimes mothers are worried and perplexed because a child of this age is so difficult at home that she does not know what to do with him, while his teacher in the Nursery School finds him charming and co-operative. The mother may comfort herself by knowing that this behaviour is caused by the sureness of the child's security in her love. He has to experiment in independence; he has to experience what happens when he does what he has been told not to do and he feels safe in so doing in his own familiar home. He does not usually fear his teacher, but he is wary of how she would react to such behaviour. He wants to retain her approval and he does not feel so secure in her affection as he does in that of his mother.

He is helped at this stage in his emotional control by his growing fluency in language. Instead of screaming in rage, throwing himself on the floor in a temper tantrum, hitting, biting and scratching, he is more likely to translate his anger and frustration into words. This is a time when he begins to use threats to other children, if he wants them to do or not to do something. Quite often his threats are totally impracticable. He will say to another child, or even to an adult, " I'll kill you ", if he cannot get his own way. These first threats are violent primitive affairs, later they will become more social, like, " I won't be your friend ", or " You can't come to my party ". The child, because he is still in the autistic stage of thinking, believes that he is all-powerful and that he can really kill. Further because of his confusion between phantasy and reality, he may unconsciously believe that because he has said " I'll kill you ", he really has done so and may suffer from guilty feelings. Therefore we as adults must always take special care to help the child to realise that this cannot happen. The child of four and five is unaware of what death and killing really mean. He may know them from television, when the " dead " man may be resuscitated in the next film, or from the death of a neighbour or relative. If it is the latter case he knows that the dead person is no longer seen about, and if it is someone he has loved he may feel again that this disappearance is his fault and he feels guilty about it. It is important that the child should express openly his fears, anger and guilty feelings as soon as he is able to do so. If he represses his feelings, or is afraid to express them, they will become more intense and violent and may result in difficult behaviour patterns, possibly withdrawing into himself, refusing to make relationships and finding difficulty in learning. He may revert to babyish patterns of behaviour in order to find the security he had in his earlier years and which he feels he has lost. These cases are not very frequent, but may be caused by a lack of facility in language when he ought to have acquired it. He can be helped by the adult who can try to clarify to him his feelings by talking about the incident to him, perhaps even joking about it if it is not concerned with the death of a real person. Children always understand more language that is spoken to them than they can use themselves.

Emotionally, therefore, the child of four to five is beginning to gain control over his emotions not only in relation to adults, but also to other children, but this brings with it the difficulty that he is more conscious of the fact when he does lose control and will be unhappy over it and again needs comforting, not scolding.

Socially, too, he is adjusting to people outside his own family, not only to other adults but also to other children. It is desirable, therefore, that he should have opportunities for meeting not only with adults, but with children of his own age for short periods of time. The child of four is not ready for long hours during which he would be under the strains and tensions which are caused by being with large numbers of other children and strange adults. He is becoming less egocentric and is beginning to play no longer alongside other children but actually with them. He is beginning to play together with small groups of two or three children and sometimes even as many as four or five. Usually these groups last for a short period of time and then the children break up and play alone by themselves until they are ready to come together again in another small group. Children find it easier to make group relationships where the games they are playing are in phantasy play and stimulate them towards co-operation. Thus Wendy-house family play, which is so popular, demands the co-operation of a father, mother and baby. Boys playing " Cowboys and Indians " need to join together in order that the game shall have meaning, and sometimes children of this age will make a co-operative effort in building with the big bricks which may then turn into a boat or a bus, which in its turn will stimulate more co-operative play. Group play at this age does not really mean the giving and taking of ideas for play. One child will take the lead and impose his ideas on other children, until another child takes the lead and without consultation imposes his ideas in turn. It is a big step forward that one child can accept the lead and ideas of another, but it is not yet the full co-operation and exchange of intellectual ideas and rules of games which only comes fully at the Junior stage. This early fluid type of co-operative play is however essential as the precursor of real group play and social involvement. Without it the child is going to find it difficult to accept the demands of the Junior group.

Intellectually, too, the child makes great strides in his development from four to five. In his language his vocabulary has more than doubled since he was three. Moreover, he is beginning to organise his language and use it more specifically. Where before the young child used his nouns generically, that is using the word " daddy' for all men, and " doggie " for all animals, now he has learnt specific names, such as uncle, postman, milkman, etc., so that he has begun not only to organise his language, but also his thoughts and ideas about his world. The world through his use of language is beginning to be more objective and less related to his own interior, egocentric world. With his appreciation of the objectiveness of the world he can just begin to realise himself as a person, to become aware of himself as a separate unique entity within the world and opposed to the other people in it. Before, everything was his, and belonged wholly to him, now he is beginning to realise that certain things belong to him, but other things belong to other people. However, unless he experiences owning something himself, something that is particularly his, he can never come to a realisation of objects belonging to other people. Children brought up in some residential homes, where all the toys are held in common so that they have no possessions of their own, find it very difficult to appreciate the fact of other people's possessions and in consequence are more likely to steal without understanding what they are doing. This realisation of other people and their belongings is an intellectual development. He is beginning to know and think in an elementary way about himself and other people. He is also beginning to use his language to satisfy his curiosity. Where before he looked, touched and tested, now he begins questions.

At first these questions are often used simply to practise his language, to show it off to adults and to receive attention, but later he begins to want to know. As his experiences are so limited the answers given to him must be within his understanding and therefore limited. One cannot give long elaborate explanations to a child of this age and he is satisfied with a short concrete practical answer. This is the period, too, when he begins to ask questions about life and death. We have already discussed the child's lack of understanding about death and how difficult it is to give him any real idea of what it means. He is naturally even more interested about birth and life, especially if he has had an experience of babies in his own family or in that of a neighbour. At this stage it is easy for him to accept the truth about birth, perhaps more than at any other period. Therefore, it is better to tell him quite frankly the simple biological facts about birth and not put him off by telling him fairy tales about gooseberry bushes or the stork or the doctor's black bag, or by putting him off by telling him that he is too young to know and that you will tell him when he is older. By doing this he is in danger of hearing later a garbled version from other children, who may have guilty feelings about having an adult secret. He in turn may develop such feelings and this may colour his attitude to sex for a long time. He must be told the truth quite simply and without embarrassment on the part of the adult. He will not understand it fully, but he will thereafter trust you and come to you for further knowledge at a later time when he is ready for it.

With his developing use of language he is also beginning to make relationships, comparisons and contrasts between objects and people. Thus a four-year-old boy, when his mother had her hair curled, said to her, " I don't like curls, my teacher hasn't got curls." Through his observation and talking about natural objects he begins to understand that from a bulb that he plants come leaves and a flower and that the hamster in the classroom sleeps and eats just as he does himself. Also, through helping to tend and look after plants, flowers and animals, he is beginning to develop a protective attitude towards things smaller than himself and to have a different perspective on the world.

Although he has advanced so much intellectually, a good many of his concepts are still very limited. Spatial relationships are only just beginning to have some meaning for him. Although he is beginning to recognise that adults are taller than he is, he still cannot use this knowledge in, for instance, his painting. He will, when painting father, mother and himself, still paint them all the same size, or himself bigger than the other two figures. He is, however, beginning to make spatial associations in that he will now usually join arms and legs to the body, put the eyes in the face and not alongside, as he may have done previously. He is beginning to use the shape of the paper for his background and place his paintings more in the centre of the paper and in some relation to one another. He is beginning also to be aware of his own limitations in space ; that he cannot reach the sky. He will get on a chair or table in order to make himself bigger and finds great pleasure in doing so. He is beginning to want to be bigger where before he was quite satisfied as he was. Although he may know the names of numbers and space concepts and may be even able to recognise the symbol of a number, he still cannot relate that number to practical experience of objects. He does not understand the " twoness " of two or the " sixness " of six. So that although we give him many experiences of naming numbers in jingles and nursery rhymes and practical experiences of pouring water, weighing objects and even as we think counting them, he still makes no relationship between the abstract concept and the practical experience. On average this will happen about the age of six and therefore it is quite illogical to expect a child under six to do arithmetical sums on paper. Although he may do them mechanically and correctly, he has no real understanding of what he is doing, and this will make the later stages in arithmetic and mathematics much more difficult for him or even incomprehensible. He has never had the real understanding of the basic principles.

We have already discussed the difficulties the child has in learning to read at an early age because of the physically difficult operation of eye-focusing, but there is also difficulty because of his lack of recognition of spatial comparisons and contrasts. He has to be able to recognise the shape of a sentence, then the shape of a word and finally the shape of letters, and until he has reached this natural maturational level of recognition he will find great difficulty in learning to read. Because of this good memory that I have already spoken about the child can quickly memorise a page of his reading book, so that if he is taught to read this page he can reproduce it at any time without necessarily understanding it. His first learning and recognition is global. That is he understands and reads a whole sentence first because it has meaning for him. Then he will come to recognise words that have meaning and these are often the bigger words. The small words are more difficult to recognise because not only are their shapes so similar, but also words like " the " have no real meaning for the child. In the same way letters have no meaning at all for the child, except perhaps as the letter that begins his own name. Therefore, it is a waste of time to teach a child his alphabet until he has gained a recognition of sentences and words. He may learn to recite the alphabet or even to recognise the names of the letters, but he will make no connection between the letters in this way and the real reading process he will go through when he is mature enough to learn to read. It must be realised that to bring pressure to bear on a child to make him read before he has reached that stage of maturity may result in his developing attitudes of dissatisfaction with, and dislike of reading, and therefore he will never read unless forced to do so. A child who is made to read and write before he is ready will often be found writing letters and numbers back to front or upside-down, showing in this way his lack of appreciation of spatial relationships and connections. It is essential, therefore, for easy learning of reading and writing that the child should have reached the necessary standard of maturity.

In the same way a child of four to five is only just beginning to develop a sense of time. Any aspects of time he knows are those connected with events which are closely related to his own way of life. He knows, for instance, that after dinner he has a rest, and, in the Nursery School, after his rest his mother will come for him to take him home. He has no idea how long that rest period is or how long after he gets up his mother will come for him. He may know the date of his birthday, but makes no connections between that date and other happenings in the year. He will hear adults say " It's time for dinner " or " It's time to go to bed " without a real understanding of the word time at all. It is just a word that adults use. But he will gradually come to make a connection between the position of the hands of a clock and certain events if the adult tells him that when the two hands of the clock stand straight up it will be dinner time. The more incidental teaching of this kind he

FIG. 1. Baby holds up his head.

FIG. 2. Baby sits erect.

FIG. 3. Widens experience through independent movement.

FIG. 4. A young child will squat for long periods.

Fig. 5. He can throw a ball.

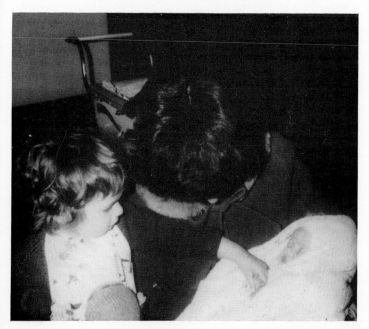

Fig. 6. Helping the child to accept the new baby.

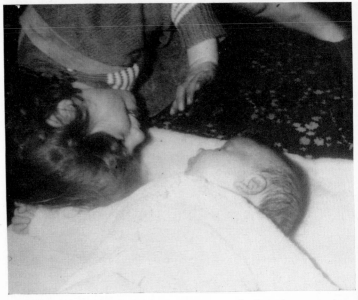

FIG. 7. She wants to find out all about it.

FIG. 8. The child is fascinated by all living things.

FIG. 9. He will play alongside other children.

FIG. 10. She can hang upside-down.

FIG. 11. Tying laces usually defeats him.

FIG. 12. He is beginning to play with other children.

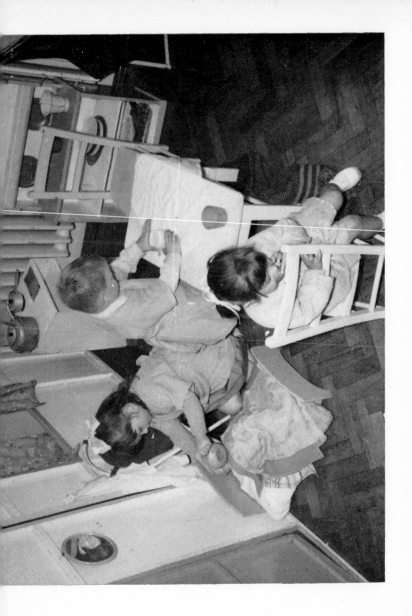

FIG. 13. He uses play to clarify his experiences.

Fig. 14. Play materials that demand collaboration.

FIG. 15. The child paints what she knows.

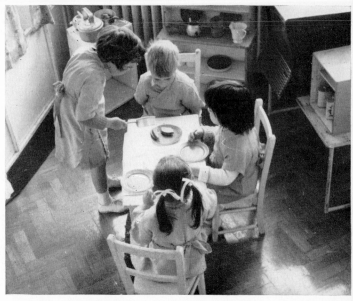

Fig. 16. Imitative play is carried out in a small group.

Fig. 17. Sand in the garden offers many opportunities.

Fig. 18. Musical experiences should be creative.

Fig. 19. The child extends his experiences in movement.

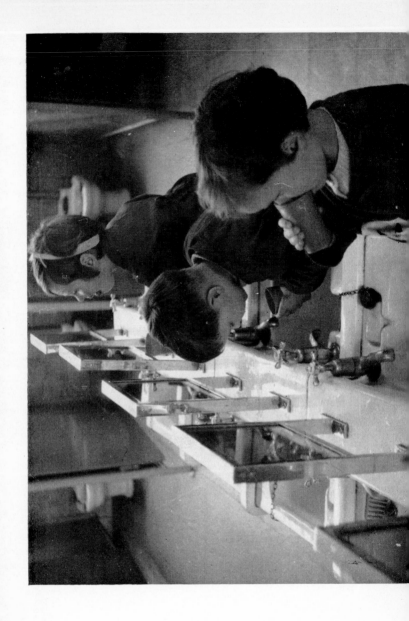

FIG. 20. Social training goes on all day long.

has the better he will be able to understand time factors when the right stage is reached. In the same way when he is told a story, although he appears to be following the sequence of events, if he is asked to repeat back the same story he will jumble up the events in time, so that in the story of Red Riding Hood, for instance, the wolf may kill the grandmother before he meets Red Riding Hood. Quite often the child will tell the most exciting, and therefore the most important, part of the story first wherever it comes in the sequence of the plot. Also his use of time phraseology is often quite inaccurate. He will say " I went there tomorrow " or " Will you come to school yesterday ? " It is only by continued time experiences and by the adult relating those experiences to the time words that they will gradually come to have real meaning for him. Again, practical experiences related to language must come before abstract manipulation of time concepts.

If the three- to five-year-old has gone through all these stages successfully in all aspects of his development; if with his mother's and father's help he has conquered all the difficulties he had to meet; and if he has had all the stimulus and encouragement for many and varied experiences in his learning, he will have developed into the delightful five-year-old we saw in the first chapter. Most of his experiences and learning at this stage have come to him through his free self-chosen play activities and therefore the values of play and the materials and opportunities we should provide will be the subject of the next chapter.

CHAPTER 5

Play. What is play? Values of play to young children. Suitable play materials.

FROEBEL has said : " Play and speech constitute the element in which the child lives."* But what is play and why do children play ? The very young baby plays with his body, with his fingers and toes, as it seems naturally, and yet if he is not encouraged and further stimulated by the adult, as we have seen in the case of the deprived child in an institution, he will cease to play and will lie quiet and passive. There have been many opinions put forward as to why children play. One view is that children and animals play because they have too much energy and that this superfluous energy must be discharged otherwise the development of the child will be harmed because there is no outlet for it. On the other hand it is well known that children and even adults will go on playing after they are tired and have obviously got rid of their superfluous energy. Another view is that play is purely imitative ; that the child plays or goes through the actions because he sees other people doing them, but although involved in many play sequences which the child follows through, this does not explain the play of the very young child. Another explanation is that a child engages in play because he has an instinctive urge to prepare himself for adult life, that he practises in play what he will need to preserve his life at a later stage. The Greeks believed this and this view has been advocated by those who have studied the play of animals (who in their play perform all the functions that help them to escape from danger and hunt for their

* Op. cit., p. 54.

food) and draw an analogy from this with human beings. But this still does not explain the random undifferentiated play of the young infant. Other views that have been put forward are that children play because they wish to get rid of harmful impulses, or that they have a need to compete with or dominate over other children. But although many of these factors enter into the play of young children, they still do not explain what play is.

Most of the advocates of these views seem to think that we need to find an excuse for play; that it must fulfil some function for adult life. They do not stress the importance of the intrinsic value of play to the child himself as a child. Yet Froebel says :

> Play is the highest phase of child development . . . of human development at this period; for it is self-active representation of the inner . . . representation of the inner, from inner necessity and impulse. Play is the purest, most spiritual activity of man at this stage, and at the same time typical of human life as a whole . . . of the inner hidden natural life in man and all things. It gives, therefore, joy, freedom, contentment, inner and outer rest, peace with the world. It holds all the sources of all that is good. A child that plays thoroughly, with self-active determination, persevering until physical fatigue forbids, will surely be a thorough determined man, capable of self sacrifice for the promotion of the welfare of himself and others . . . As already indicated, play at this time is not trivial, it is highly serious and of deep significance.*

So Froebel believed that play has an intrinsic value of its own; that there is within the child an urgent necessity to play and that through his play he is evolving his own inner life and destiny. He believed that play is the child's work, and work the child's play; and that moreover if he does not work hard at his play and concentrate with all his strength on the immediate play activity, he will not as a man be able to concentrate fully and with all his strength on his work.

The child therefore gains most of his education through his play, but because at this stage he unconsciously knows what is best for himself his play must be self-chosen and self-directed. However, although his play must be in the first place self-chosen, he has had very little experience of life and therefore does not know how to

*Op. cit., pp. 54–55.

extend his play further. The adult here must step in and show him how to go on to new experiences so that he gets the full value from his first impulse to play. It is the most skilled mother or other adult who realises when the child's interest is about to flag, to understand when he has got the greatest value from his own self-directed play and so step in and suggest extensions to that play, giving him new ideas and experiences. But if the child has taken in as much as he can from the original interest and is not ready for an extension of it, which may happen if he has not reached that stage of maturity, he will either ignore the suggestion and go on to a completely new interest, or he may attempt to follow the suggestion and fail to get any value from it. Play imposed by the adult without the child's *full* co-operation and involvement will probably do more harm than good to the child. The sensitivity and understanding of the adult is therefore vital when dealing with the pre-school child in his play activities. She must not only be aware of when the child is losing interest in one activity, but also of when he is getting physically and mentally tired and simply wants to relax, preferably on his mother's lap, and let life and experiences flow over him. After a period of fierce mental and physical activity he must have time to assimilate and make completely his own those experiences he has gone through before he is ready to add to them, either by more parallel experiences, extensions of the old ones, or completely new ones, but he must get the full value from each experience by assimilation before he goes on to the next one.

What specific values do we expect very young children to get from their play experiences and what types of play are common to them and provide the best means for all-round development? How can the home provide the best materials and stimuli for a child's play as the main source of his education in all aspects of development? Physically he begins to learn very early the control of his limbs; he learns co-ordination between mind and muscle. The first random play of the baby, the waving and pushing of arms and legs in the air, should be encouraged and helped by freedom from tight clothing and short periods of play on a bed or a rug where he has all the space in the world to get the feeling of the movement of his limbs. Soon he needs something to grasp, so that he can wave it about and bang it on the nearest object, and so unconsciously become aware of his feelings of power over an object that is an extension of himself. If that object is one like a rattle that makes a noise, he gets an even greater feeling of power and enjoyment over this object. It is his first unconscious realisation of himself as an object in the world with attachment to other objects in that world. He is also learning mentally through the objects that are given to him to play with, though this learning is not conscious yet. He is learning about the different qualities of objects presented to him. That some are hard, some are soft, especially in his mouth ; some are solid like a cube and some are hollow like a ring. Therefore the baby should be given an increasing variety of such toys as he gets older. These need not be elaborate expensive toys from shops, but the baby likes them brightly coloured. They should be un-differentiated in their use, that is, to be used in many ways by the child, thus a ring can be used by the child for feeling, putting in his mouth and sucking, can be easily passed from one hand to another, so helping hand–eye co-ordination, or can be strung up over the baby's cot or pram for him to follow with his eyes or to clutch at with his hands. In the same way small wooden cubes, which can easily be made by a father, can be used in numberless ways by a child. As he gets older and begins to crawl around the floor he needs more objects which will roll or slide so that he is encouraged to go after them ; as soon as he begins to walk he will find a simple truck which he can push and pull helps him with his balance and feeling of confidence in his own powers of locomotion. If this is a good solid truck on four wheels with a sturdy handle, it can, as the child grows older, be used in a great variety of ways. The child will use it to put things in and take them out again. A child of eighteen months or two years will spend endless time just putting in and taking out, finding tremendous satisfaction in so doing. He will use the truck for transporting things from one place to another as his horizons widen, and as he gets

still older for his dolls or soft toys. Later when he comes to play
with a companion they will take turns at having a ride in it and so
help their social development. This is just one example of one
piece of equipment which, if chosen well and strongly made, will
be used by the child to meet his differing needs at each stage of
development.

When buying or making toys for children they should always be
thought of in terms of the variety of uses to which they may be
put as well as of their durability. At the pre-school stage the child
does not need the carefully exact model of an aeroplane in plastic
which will break very quickly and cause him frustration and sorrow.
He is much happier with two pieces of wood which he himself has
nailed together and called an aeroplane, with which he will go
zooming round the room. The same " aeroplane " may turn at any
moment into a sword to be used in a dramatic fight, and this meets
the child's immediate and changing needs in a way in which no
fragile toy from a shop can. The children will always show us what
is right if we know how to look for it and give them a chance.

As the child grows older he meets more and more experiences
which he cannot understand and more objects to deal with which
he wants to know more about. So in the first place he uses play to
clarify his experiences. These activities at first are unaccompanied
by language. They are sensory experiences and a young child as
already described will feel, smell and taste everything to find out
about its qualities, but he cannot have abstract ideas about them
until he has attained the use of language. However, the more of
this preliminary exploration he does before he is ready to express
it in language, the greater will be his ability to put all his
experiences into language when that stage of maturity is reached.
The child with few pre-language experiences will be the child who
is slow in language development. As he acquires some language
ability he will begin to accompany his play with a running commentary, " Me do this ", " now water ", " now sand ", etc. This
speech is not addressed to anyone, it is monologue form, but the
child is more likely to engage in it if a sympathetic adult is nearby,

to whom he may at any moment address himself. By this translating his actions into words as he does them, the child is beginning to build up mental concepts of what before were only sensory experiences, and as he does so he clarifies objects to himself and will in time begin to organise his concepts into groups and patterns of thought. This vital learning will best be achieved by the child through play, chosen by the child and not directed. This clarification and understanding will, however, still be on the child's own level, not an adult one. One has only to think of this in relation to size. What to an adult would be a very small piece of apparatus would appear to a child a very large object in relation to his own size. A great many adults have had the experience of returning to a place where they had been as children and been surprised to find how everything has shrunk and become much smaller than their memory of it. So this mental learning is still at a childish stage and we must be aware of this and make allowances for the child's lack of adult understanding, though he may appear to understand us at our own level. Phantasy is very strong in the child at this age. He does not only imitate adults in his play, but identifies himself so completely with them that, for the time being, he actually is the father or mother, the postman or coalman, or aeroplane pilot, and so begins to feel what he considers the power of the adult over everything in his world. Through playing out the actions of adults he begins to get a childish understanding of them which will satisfy his wonder and confusion for the moment. This attempt at understanding adults will develop more on the intellectual level when he comes to the stage when he can manipulate mental concepts. The understanding he has created for himself is still on the autistic level of his own world of thinking, of adults' actions in relation to himself and in his own particular world.

As well as clarification of physical experiences the child will attempt to solve through his play his emotional difficulties and so come to terms with them. As we have said, as the young child becomes less dependent on his mother he meets with many frustrating emotional experiences, and any frustrating emotional experience may bring with it feelings of guilt. When his mother goes into hospital he unconsciously feels it is because of something he has done. When he feels jealousy for the father–mother relationship, this carries with it very strong guilty feelings. He cannot express these feelings in words, partly because he has not the ability in words and partly because the intensity of the feeling forbids its expression in case through expressing it he does harm to himself. So he finds the necessary clarification and diminution of strength of feeling through his play. In his play he becomes the strong father figure whom he so much admires and who, he is unconsciously sure, could never have feelings of guilt. He transfers to himself through identification the strength of his father and so conquers his own guilty feelings. In his play he does the things his father does, or the things he thinks he does. He goes to work, he goes down to the pub for some beer, and with the co-operation of another child he orders the " mother " about, tells her to get his dinner ready for him. He will also tell the " children " to sit down and behave, but is usually tender to the " baby " of the family. By playing out the family relationships he is beginning to come to an understanding of them and of his own place in the family community, and will also demonstrate to himself his own power, for a short time, to conquer his childish feelings.

In the same way a little girl will play the mother's role. She will in her turn order the father to eat his dinner or go to work or give her some money for the shopping. She will order the children about and at times be very harsh with them. This is very often the sign that she is unconsciously harbouring guilty feelings and feels that she should be treated harshly and punished for her supposed badness. At any moment, however, having punished her children, she will be kind and gentle to them, which is what she as a child most desires from her own mother. It is interesting to note that either boy or girl will be either father or mother. Any child may at any time wish to be of the opposite sex and finds wish-fulfilment in phantasy play. The wish to change sex comes more obviously where a child has heard a chance remark by parents or neighbours such as, " What a pity she's not a boy ", and the remark may stay with the child until he or she builds up a picture of rejection by the parents, as we have seen always a paramount fear at this age. In the same way a small boy who has been over-protected by his parents, particularly by his mother, may wish to be a girl, who seems to have a greater right to such protection than a boy. Also the small girl may envy the freedom given to her brother, although this is usually a later development, and so wish to be a boy. Moreover, a small girl as we have seen has a great admiration for her father and may wish to resemble him more closely. These are natural wishes evolving from the child's growing realisation of the family situation and in free phantasy play the child will be the person he wishes to be without interference and without feelings of guilt. Once he has gained satisfaction from having really been the person he wanted to be and having been in complete control of the situation, he is able to come back to a happy acceptance of the situation as it really is.

One of the other difficulties which many children have and which we have already mentioned is that of the new baby in the home and the natural jealousy, anger and guilty feelings which come to the older child. Children who are given the chance will in turn play out this situation. A child will find relief from tensions through being the dominant mother figure. Very often he smacks the doll who represents the baby, throws it about violently, casts it away from him and rejects it, just what he would like his mother to do to the intruder in the family. He can do this safely with no harm to himself. He may find the same release from emotional troubles by playing with the baby tenderly and gently, mothering it and thus showing his superiority over the situation. On the other hand he may find his release by being the baby in his play. He may allow himself to be bullied by another child as the mother figure, and does not protest. In this way he is punished for his angry feelings as the second child, which to him is right and proper and therefore gives him relief, or he is being treated in a loving way as he would like his baby to be treated if his feelings would allow him. This is an age when ambivalence of emotional reaction predominates and he shows this by his swing from anger to gentleness, dominance to submission, in his play. An important point to remember when thinking about these play situations is that the child himself is master of the whole situation; he is in charge of it, so that if at any time his aggression becomes too violent and frightens him, he can bring the whole play to a stop and become something quite different, or become again his mother's small boy looking for comfort and protection from her.

Another way in which children are helped in their emotional development through phantasy is through the playing out of fears, real and imaginary. I have mentioned the predominant fear of the young child of being rejected or deserted by his mother, but there are other specific fears which have arisen from actual happenings or through stories told to them or seeing films in the cinema or on television. Any children who have had experience of hospitals, even if it is only for a day or two, carry with them very strong memories of being left in a strange place by their mothers where unpleasant things are done to them. However good the hospital may be, it is still a terrifying situation for a child; the size of the building alone can be frightening. In the same way he may relate feeling pain with a visit to doctor and dentist. Children cannot understand these situations; they cannot see what it is for. However much the adult may explain, they cannot wholly accept the explanation. In order to get this understanding they play it out in phantasy. Many Nursery Schools realise the need to promote this play and provide for the children's use, nurses' aprons and caps, a doctor's bag, a miniature stethoscope made from rubber tubing, and a bed where a patient may lie. Any given child may be in turn patient, doctor or nurse and so come to a greater understanding, at their own level, of the frightening situation. Again, as they are in command of the play they can stop it if it becomes too frightening for them to take. Other frightening experiences can be helped in the same way by the provision of dressing-up clothes.

Adults often wonder why children join in games where they are chased shrieking across the garden or room, but if they are playing out their fears in a phantasy role, from which they can escape at any time, it will help them to realise that their fears are not all-powerful and that they can come to terms with them. Even very young children will play at ghosts or burglars without having any idea what either is. They will put a cloth over their heads and say, " I'm a ghost ", and all the other children will run away, but if one asks them what a " ghost " is, they do not know. It is an overall term, as so many words that children use are, which they have heard adults or older children use, and which covers anything that is frightening. One Nursery School child painted quite a recognisable bear and said it was a ghost ! By playing out a ghost or a burglar a child can demonstrate to himself his powers over these frightening entities and so come to terms with these fears of the unknown. There are so many " unknowns " at this stage of life and all of them may contain aspects which to the child are frightening. They pick up very quickly words and feelings related to those words both from adults and even more significantly from older children. Often through misconception they attach fears to words which have no fear element in them and adults may tell them not to be ridiculous.

So many fears appear to us quite irrational, and yet many of those fears last right through into adult life. Why, for instance, are so many adults still afraid of the dark ? Besides demonstrating his power over the fearful person, object or situation, the child comes through his identification with it in phantasy, into some understanding of it, still at his own level. He does, however, quite often need an adult's help over this. A small Nursery child was terrified because he was convinced that there was a " bogy-man " in the electric light fuse box, high up on the wall. He refused to lie down and have his rest in case the bogy-man got him while he was asleep, until the adult climbed up and opening the box showed him what it contained. The adult can tell the child not to be afraid and try to explain, but because language comprehension is so limited it is better, if possible, to give a practical demonstration. I think, perhaps, at this stage it is unwise for the adult to join in the frightening game with the child. Sometimes, particularly with a very sensitive and imaginative child, he becomes over-involved in the play emotionally and cannot get rid of it, and here the adult has to bring him back to reality in her own real person. She has to rescue him from his own phantasies and therefore must remain in the reality world as mother or teacher.

One is very much aware of how much children play imitatively. They imitate adults' behaviour and adult feelings as they imagine them to be. The child has found in his baby life that when he imitates his mother in any way she approves of what he is doing and therefore he associates pleasure with imitative activity and continues to imitate. It may be real life imitation, as in helping mother to sweep the floor or dust, or there may be a phantasy element in it as we have seen, in playing out roles of father or mother. A young child always wants to be like the adults he likes, and wants to do what they do. This brings him in his own mind into closer companionship with them and he feels less on an inferior level. The small child in the adult world gains for a few moments the level of equality and this makes him feel more confident and superior. This kind of work-play is therefore important to the child. It may be very trying for the mother to have to wait while the child does something which she could do ten times more quickly herself, but his pleasure and delight will make up to her for the time she has lost. Therefore in the home every opportunity should be made to afford the child opportunities to help. It is important, too, to help a child to do a thing correctly even in his play. He enjoys being completely successful, but because he is so immature and his muscles have not yet attained full co-ordination he does find difficulty in, for instance, sweeping up dust. So the adult must help him to finish it off to a proper standard and not just accept any kind of performance because he is so small. He himself thinks that he can do anything successfully and he will be aware of it if allowances are made for him, and will feel frustrated. We must give him the full satisfaction of finishing a job correctly. An individual child will play imitatively by himself as when, for instance, a boy knocks a nail into a piece of wood and says, " Daddy does it like this " or a little girl bathing her doll will say, " Mummy does it like this." This is direct imitation without identification and has a purpose of its own to fulfil. This is perhaps the beginnings of taking an objective view of the world. " Mummy " and " Daddy " are no longer people simply belonging to himself; they are personalities with lives of their own. The child is standing outside of himself and observing what goes on without being involved in it. This is a great step forward in his progress, but he still has a long way to go before he comes to the stage of full self-consciousness, a full realisation of himself in relation to the rest of the world. The child, however, while playing in this way, will sometimes talk to an adult about it because he still needs her support. He is not yet confident enough to stand on his own although he is beginning to take an objective standpoint.

Other imitative plays are carried out by young children in small groups of two or three and therefore are very valuable in promoting the child's social development. As we have seen, the very young child is completely egocentric, but there comes a time when, in his natural maturation, he is ready to make social contacts with other children. The first of these contacts are usually made in phantasy play, when the child in his identified role needs another child to play a complementary identified role, and because they are not playing in their own identities they can bear to adjust to one another in a phantasy social situation. The next step is for two children to play deliberately together in an imitative situation, being aware of their own personalities while imitating others. For example, two little girls parading round a Nursery classroom, dressed in bridal clothes, said, " We're getting married ", and then one added, " We can't really, 'cos she's a girl, too." She had grasped the reality fact that a boy and a girl are needed for a wedding, but in an imitating, pretending play, it did not matter.

If a child is to live a happy and successful life, able to adjust to the community in which he lives, able to make relationships with other people, accept other people's points of view and accept limitations placed upon him by society, as an individual for the good of that society, he must learn at the right moment in his maturational pattern how to make social relationships. This must be at the right moment for each individual child, and it happens in the first place through play, but only if the right stimuli for that kind of play are provided. As we have seen, he plays socially first in phantasy play, next in imitative play, and finally in reality play on the child's own level. Play materials that demand the collaboration of another child must be provided, so that the incentive for such play comes through the child's own interest in and choice of material. Once he has chosen the material and started to play with it, he then finds that he needs someone to help him. For instance, one will see a child in a Nursery School trying to build a bus or a train from large boxes. They are too big for a child to cope with, so he calls another child to help him and from there they proceed to give one another proposals and ideas. Quite often there is a good deal of opposition to one another's ideas, " No, don't put it there ", or " It doesn't go there ", and sometimes a certain amount of aggression, but usually a dominant leader emerges, and a social pattern evolves of leader and led. One child prefers to lead ; another to follow.

Sometimes the social pattern is formed by one child becoming interested in what another child is doing and either joins in without an invitation, or may ask, " Can I play ? " Again this shows a marked development in the child's accepting the fact that the play situation is the property of another child ; that he himself does not own everything and that he must get the other child's consent before joining in. Sometimes the child who is already playing will reject the request. He does not want interference from that particular child and in an advanced stage of development will choose one child and reject another, and these are valuable learning points for both children. The fact has not yet been made consciously obvious to them that they can be accepted or rejected, and in most cases they have always been accepted. Construction materials of this sort are therefore useful and in the same way the child will find that playing with a ball and even more with a bat and ball is more fun if two children play together. One must still accept the fact, however, that children of this age are still egocentric and still need solitary, individual play. They will move rapidly from playing alone to social play and back again to solitary play. It still imposes a certain strain on the child to give and take with another; it is still strange to him to take turns with another child, and it is still frustrating to him to see another child doing what he wants to do himself. So we should only expect such social play to last for a short time and we would expect the constitution of the group to change frequently, as one child drops out and another one comes in. These preliminary small interchanging groups are the prelude to the formation of the later gangs of the Junior School, and if the child is successful in these early attempts at social interchange, he is much more likely to make a good social adjustment later. Therefore the adult must do everything possible to help the continuance of such social play. By a suggestion or a hint or a new piece of apparatus she may be able to start off a new play progression which will keep the group together for a longer time just when it was ready to break up. The more such play becomes habitual to the child, the more likely he is to continue with it and extend it.

A young child naturally tends to be aggressive. In his very early life, as we have seen, he is being constantly frustrated in his efforts to do what he wants, as what he wants is not acceptable, quite often, to the adults and does not fit into the pattern of the adult culture in which he is living. He is prevented from doing what he wants to do and shows his frustration and anger by aggressive behaviour in an attempt to force his will on the adult and prove himself powerful. He has sometimes found that such aggressive behaviour gains him what he wants, when the frustrated adult in turn gives way to him. If he finds that this happens he will obviously repeat the pattern of behaviour. Even if he is not allowed to do the forbidden thing, his aggressive behaviour still gains him the adult's attention, and this is what he is constantly seeking. These aggressive feelings are important to the child, for without them he would not progress very far in his development. From them he gets energy and driving power for his learning, so what we have to do as adults is to provide him with materials and circumstances through which his aggression can be used in a positive socially acceptable way, rather than in anti-social ways. Through the materials we provide he must be able to develop feelings of power, a subconscious awareness that he is able, through his own power, to control these very intense aggressive feelings which frighten him as much as they may do his mother. His aggressive feelings usually result in physical attacks, and therefore we must give him the opportunity of making such physical attacks on materials. A piece of clay which he can pound and bang and thump can be used by the child to get rid of his feelings. A hammer which is heavy enough to drive nails satisfactorily into a piece of wood, or a hammer toy with pegs which can be hit forcefully to drive them into holes, are all helpful. A piece of dough from mother's baking is more satisfactory to the younger child than clay as it is more easily moulded by less developed hand muscles. Paint can be splashed on to paper regardless of the end product ; water can be poured endlessly from container to bowl or from one container to another, and sand can be used in numberless ways to demonstrate one's power over it. The child must be allowed to use the materials as he pleases, but he must also be made aware that he does so with the adult's full approval. Therefore the adults must take precautionary measures so that the child does not have any guilty feelings about his aggressive play. By this I mean that he must be given a plastic overall which can be easily wiped while he is playing with water or paint or clay, so that he has no fears about getting wet or dirty. Tables or floors should be covered with plastic covers or newspaper, again to prevent the child from feeling guilty about making a mess. The use of materials must be made easy for him ; that is they must be at hand at the moment of frustration or anger when he wants them. I watched a small boy trying to make an aeroplane out of two pieces of wood. He struggled for a long time without success, becoming more and more tensed up and frustrated. He refused the adult help that was offered because he was determined to do it by himself.

In the end he was so thoroughly frustrated and angry that he threw it down and went over to the painting easel. There he picked up a brushful of paint and rubbed it violently all over the paper, so violently that he nearly made a hole in the paper. He then put the brush back in the paint pot, went back to the woodwork table and quietly finished his aeroplane. He had found the solution to his problem, because he could think calmly and unemotionally about it.

It is obviously more difficult in the home situation to provide the wealth of suitable materials to be found in the Nursery School, or the space in which always to leave them available for the child, but one can be aware of when a child is becoming frustrated by the activity he is attempting and put something else out for him or suggest something which might meet his difficulties. This aggressive destructive type of play is most necessary to a young child, but at the same time it is necessary that he should develop through destructive play to constructive play. His aggressive bashing and banging, breaking up and knocking down to relieve his frustrations and tensions do not give him the feelings of satisfaction that he gets from having made something. Therefore when the child has worked out his aggressive feelings in this way, it is our job as adults to suggest ways to him, or show him ways, of making something. And so we come to creative play.

It may seem absurd to talk of creative work or play by a pre-school child, but we must realise that at a very early age he does start to create. Perhaps the first creative work he does is in sound. At first he experiments with sounds, trying them out, and then very shortly, even before he can speak intelligibly, he takes great delight in deliberately using syllables to make a variety of sounds. This is his first aesthetic use of sound language and he will go on later, after he has learned to speak, still using nonsense syllables. He will make a triumphant chant with an occasional recognisable word, to celebrate his success in building or making. Sometimes a group of four-year-old children, having made a high tower from bricks, will walk or dance round it chanting, just as warriors celebrated their victories in war by strong rhythmic patterns of song. This joy is creative and should be further stimulated by the adult's approving appreciation so that the child will gradually come to create songs and chants of success in real words. At this time the child uses his whole body to create movement to accompany his songs. After the creation of sounds and movement, which if the child is left free will be rhythmic, fitting into the pattern of each child's individual rhythm, he will go on to create rhythmic patterns for himself on suitable instruments. These instruments can mostly be made at home quite easily and are usually better than the toy instruments bought in the shop for the young child. Shakers which give different sounds can be made from tin or cardboard cartons, filled with such things as dried peas or beans, rice, barley, etc., and firmly stuck down. Good drums can be made by fastening a piece of inner tubing from a motor tyre over the open end of a tin. These can be made in different sizes to give different sounds and can be struck either by hand or with a drumstick. Bells are attractive to children. These can be small bells fastened to a stick or circle of wire, or bell sounds can be obtained from cutting different lengths of copper or steel to give different notes. One can make a complete scale from these and they can be suspended from a string or placed in a stand and played with a drumstick. Different notes can be obtained from jam-jars, filled to different levels with water. All these will produce a satisfactory tune or melody for the child. Clappers made from different types of wood can be used by the child to produce simple percussion rhythms or to produce different sounds from the different woods. A child should also, whenever possible, be given the chance to experiment with adult instruments such as piano, guitar, pipes, xylophone, etc., but here I think one should help the child by showing him how to use the instrument, for instance that a piano should be played with the fingers and not the palm of the hand, in order that he may get the fullest value from the experience. His mother singing to him or with him will help him, first to imitate her alone, and later to hum or sing phrases and tunes which may have as a base those which he has already heard, but also to create individual interpretations and additions.

In order to create music, he will need a great many experiences in listening to music. He will probably hear plenty of popular music from radio, television, gramophone, or from older brothers and sisters, but they are at this age very catholic in their tastes and we should therefore try to give them a wide variety. Some of the modern composers, whom some adults find difficult to take and enjoy, are readily accepted and enjoyed by very young children, because their musical taste has not yet been conditioned. They also show great delight in classical music either to listen to or move to. It is easy to see from their faces, as well as from what they say, what music they like. There is no pretence at liking the music they think you want them to like as there might be at a later stage. Even at this stage it is not too early to let them experience the relationship between music symbols and the actual experience of heard music. Just as the child sees print and pretends to read it, before he can really read, so one would provide music books for him to look at. There are attractive nursery rhyme books with pictures and music which children thoroughly enjoy. In a Nursery School one often sees a child take a music book, prop it up on the stand and " play " the music on the piano and sing to it according to his interpretation. This familiarity with musical notation will help him later when he is learning to read music properly. If a child is given notes, cut out in the shape of crotchets, to play with and to place as he pleases on a piece of paper or flannel graph, the adult can then play his tune to him on an instrument to further increase his interest in music notation. At a later stage this will develop into placing notes on a stave, but at the pre-school stage this would only confuse the child. It is the creating of music in play either through movement or on an instrument that is vital at this stage, but this must be accompanied by wide experience of all kinds of music. A child is naturally rhythmic, but we can kill his natural rhythm only too quickly if we impose on the child at too early a stage adult concepts of tune and rhythm. He must be free to develop his own in his own way. We may not help to create a Beethoven or Mozart in this way, but we will help an individual to develop who is aware of the variety and beauty of sound, and who is confident in attempting to create or reproduce sound and rhythm, and the best way to do this is through the child's play.

Froebel has said : " The faculty of drawing is . . . as much innate in the child, in man, as is the faculty of speech, and demands its development and cultivation as imperatively as the latter ; experience shows this clearly in the child's early love for drawing, in the instinctive desire for drawing."* Drawing, therefore, is as important to the child as speech. They are both forms of expression and communication. Facility in drawing develops later than facility in speech, as it takes longer for the child to learn the control of hand and finger muscles and to learn the hand-eye co-ordination which are necessary for the practice of drawing, than to learn control over the organs of speech. Also drawing is not as necessary for the child's preservation of life as is speech. But at the same time the child can, if given the opportunity, express himself more adequately and fluently through drawing in the pre-school stage, once he has gained the necessary control, than he can in speech. He cannot express in words his emotional disturbances, his feelings of guilt and aggression, but the trained adult can decipher such feelings from his drawings. A child will sometimes get relief from his feelings by painting, but because his unconscious feelings of guilt are so strong he cannot allow his paintings to be seen by the adult, and so he will hurriedly paint over what he has done. Art for the child has two functions, as has speech. First it has aesthetic value as a creative art, and second communication, communication of his feelings, and communication of his intellectual development. There is a resemblance between the developmental stages of speech and drawing. The unco-ordinated babbling of the young baby trying out his speech organs resembles the scribbling of the young artist. Attempts are at first tentative, so one gets one syllable from the child and one tiny scribble, often in the corner of the paper. The random pronunciation of a recognisable syllable resembles the random formation of a space enclosed by lines which is then

*Op. cit., p. 79.

recognised as something by the child, *after* he has made it. The global representation of a shape is like the generic use of nouns, and finally we have the more specific representation of objects both in speech and art, though this stage will appear later in art than in speech. The most important factors in the development of the child's ability to draw are that he should be left free, free to draw in his own way, never being made to copy, or being told something is wrong, and free to draw at the time when he wants to. There are no " art periods " in the Nursery School. The materials are there for the child to use, as and when he pleases.

The values of free art work to the child are very great. In the first place he can express his own individuality as all great artists do, and in expressing that individuality he will come gradually to appreciate himself and his own value as a personality, distinct and yet with relationships with other people. He finds that he has power over the material; he can do what he pleases with it. He may paint with great blobs of colour, one only, and feel he has created something wonderful for himself. He may then experiment with two or three colours and the result is even more colourful and exciting. Then he may in this free painting or drawing make a shape which he recognises as something he knows and to which he can give a name, and so makes his first attempt to give a name to a symbol which he himself has made.

This is a tremendous advance in his intellectual development. Further, it has been found that children who paint and draw a lot do appear to develop a greater facility in speech. A small four-year-old boy was referred to a Nursery School by a Child Guidance Clinic, because his speech was practically non-existent; he only communicated at about the level of an eighteen-month-old child. For about three months he would not join in any of the Nursery activities except painting. He was quiet and gentle, interfered with no one and seemed quite happy and contented as long as he could paint, and his paintings were of a very advanced level for his stage of development. This showed that it was not any backwardness in intellectual ability that was holding up his speech development

After these three months, without any kind of pressure being brought to bear, he began to speak quite naturally and correctly at the level of the other children of his chronological age. He still continued to paint frequently, but more and more joined in activities with other children. As with dramatic, phantasy, and imitative play, so the child through his painting comes to a greater understanding of the world around him. If he paints a house, the house is small and so within his grasp of reality. If he puts people in his house they also are small and so within his power, and he can begin to realise the relationship between people and houses and between other objects that he paints. This establishment of relationships is one of the most important factors in the intellectual development of the child and has real meaning for the child when he has established them for himself. These relationships are still at a childish level. The child will draw what he knows, not what he sees. Thus because he knows he is the most important person, when he is doing a painting of his family, very often he will make himself the biggest person in his picture. In drawing a man the head is drawn very very large, often with only legs to accompany it, and in the face, eyes and mouth come long before a nose is added. A child of this age therefore cannot copy an object or drawing by someone else unless it fits into his own concept of the object, or drawing of it.

In order to help the child to get the full value from his drawing activities, although we will not attempt to get him to copy anything or paint anything specific to our desire, we can help him by supplying him with all the necessary materials for his work. It is not always possible in the home to give him all the materials available in the Nursery School, but we can provide him with the *right* materials. If a home-made easel with a shelf in front to hold the paint pots is available, that is most economical of space. Otherwise newspaper spread on the floor is usually the best situation for a child. A plastic cover which can be easily cleaned is even better as it is labour-saving. Paper should be large enough for a child to spread his picture well : about one foot by two is a good size. Any kind of paper is interesting and satisfying to the child. A roll of kitchen paper goes a very long way and is cheap. Wrapping paper off parcels gives the child experiences of different textures and different colours, and shows him the different responses of the paint to the different textures. Books of old wallpaper patterns give a child great pleasure, whether he paints on the right side and tries to follow the pattern, or paints freely on the wrong side. Paper bags which contained the shopping can be cut open and used on the inside; usually the outside is too shiny to take paint properly. As a last resort, newspaper itself can be used, although this is not so satisfactory as the printing makes it difficult for the child to see what he is doing, but it is better than nothing.

For the paint itself, the best, most easily used, is powder paint, which is now used in most Primary Schools. If half-pound jars of the three primary colours are obtained, a little of these can be ready mixed for the child. It is more economical to mix only a little at a time, as children may experiment with mixing colours and are left with a dirty brown in each jar. Small jars should have a larger base than top to prevent easy tipping over, but the top should be wide enough for the child to get the brush in easily. If possible, different sizes of brushes are desirable so that the child should have different experiences of manipulation, but if only one is provided this should be a large one with a handle that is easy to grasp, particularly in the early stages when the child will use an overhand grasp and use his whole shoulder and arm to manipulate it. The four-to five-year-olds will find pleasure and excitement in using other tools for painting, like feathers, a small piece of rag, a toothbrush, or a piece of sponge, preferably stuck on to the end of a large cork.

Hands are the tools when using " finger paint ". This can be bought ready mixed, but is rather expensive, and quite as good a result can be obtained by mixing an ordinary flour and water paste with paint which will flow easily on to the paper but is just thick enough so that when a child moves his fingers through it, it leaves a pattern which remains quite clear to be seen. For finger painting he will need either thick paper or a plastic surface. When he has finished his painting on the plastic surface, he will smooth it over and begin over and over again. One can take a " print " of it by placing a thin piece of paper over it and smoothing over it gently. He is always excited and pleased by the print and it is a new experience to transfer one result of his creative work to another medium. Finger painting does, however, need adult supervision as it tends to be rather messy, although it is very easily washed off. One would deplore very much the buying of cheap boxes of paint, with a large number of not very good colours and a cheap brush. In using such materials the child is often frustrated in his creative efforts. It is a difficult process to wet a brush with just enough water, then to rub the brush on the paint and so to transfer it to paper. He is held up by all these activities from getting on with his painting when his full concentration is on it. Everything must be easy for his immediate use. By providing him with so many colours, as I have said, so often inferior, he is prevented from the adventure of experimenting in the mixing of his own colours and getting the result he individually wants.

Such paint experiences as potato prints, lino cuts, or wax and paint pictures are not suitable for the under five-year-old. Such pattern-making needs the foresight to know beforehand what you are going to make to be a really valuable experience, and this fore-sight the child has not yet developed. He paints for the sake of painting, not in order to have an end product. This is a later stage of which Froebel says : " What formerly the child did only *for the sake of the activity*, the boy now does *for the sake of the result* or the product of his activity."* It is true that one does get an occasional child who definitely sets out to paint something at this stage, but this is the exception.

The child under five also likes to draw, though to my mind this has not as much value creatively as painting has. He cannot get the free untrammelled sweep of the brush and paint and his drawing is necessarily more linear than blocks of colour. It does, however, give the child a different medium to work and experiment with and

*Op. cit., p. 99.

he may come gradually to compare and contrast the two experiences —always a valuable intellectual exercise. Again, these experiences must be made as easy as possible for the child. A thick black pencil which easily produces satisfactory marks is better than a niggling small hard one, which is always breaking and will tend to tear the paper with the all-out pressure of the small child. Fat wax crayons with a limited number of good colours also give him different experiences of texture and colour. Chalk crayons are difficult to use as they break easily, smudge easily and are messy to use. Paper should be large enough to get as wide a sweep of pencil or crayon as possible, and fairly thick paper with a roughish surface is more rewarding than thin shiny paper, but even this is better than nothing. One advantage of drawing over painting to the busy mother is that drawing needs far less supervision. The child can be left to get on on his own with an occasional word of encouragement and praise, and by providing him with the right paper and implements he is less likely to draw on walls or other undesirable places.

Another creative activity which the child finds exciting and pleasurable and which promotes many skills and intellectual development, is cutting and sticking. The materials needed are a largish sheet of paper, some pages out of a magazine (not a *whole* magazine, as this might encourage the child to cut pages out of books), a pair of blunt-ended scissors which are sharp enough to cut easily (not plastic scissors, which are rarely sharp), and a jar of glue or paste with an easily manipulated brush or applicator. The child may be shown at first how to cut out figures or objects in advertisements or pictures, and then stick them on to his sheet of paper, which may be any colour or texture. As he experiments and practises he will become more adept at cutting, which is a difficult skill for small hands, and will gradually come to envisage his sheet of paper as the background for his picture. In this way he will begin to get some idea of spatial relationships and begin to realise that placing his cut-outs in a certain position will help to organise them into a picture. This is the prelude to the later stage of making collage pictures from pieces of material, coloured paper and so on. Children under four cannot usually manage this cutting out and sticking, but with the four-year-old it is the preliminary experience which is necessary for the fullest satisfaction in the activity at a later stage.

As well as these creative experiences in the flat we must give them creative experiences in three dimensions. For the very young child dough, made from flour and water with salt added to help to keep it fresh, and coloured with powder paint to make it look attractive, is a very good medium. If it is of the right consistency, not too wet and not too dry, it is light and easily handled. The child will first experiment with it, pushing it and pulling it, and will shortly come to making things with it, at first quite by chance.

In these early stages no implements are needed. Hands are the best tools to use, but as the child becomes satisfied with the experimenting stage he may want cutters, rollers and different shaped patty pans or cake tins. He will no longer get enough challenge from using hands only for dough and will need instruments as well. For the three-and-a-half to five-year-old clay presents a greater challenge and is, therefore, a more satisfying medium. Clay must be of the right consistency. It can be bought as powdered clay and mixed with water or it can be bought ready made up. In order to be most effective it must be kept damp, and this can be done by wrapping it in a wet cloth and keeping it in a plastic bag, but it must not be too wet or it is most frustrating for the child. As before in the beginnings of his work with clay, the child's best implements are his hands. Often he shows an initial distaste for the feel of the clay, particularly if stress has been laid on the fact that he must not get dirty, but once with encouragement he has got over this phase, he will go ahead with pummelling and thumping, pushing and pulling, until he has found out about the capabilities of clay, and from there he will go on to creating things with it. If he does not make something by chance and then give it a name, he may need a suggestion from the adult when he is tired of just experimenting.

There comes a time when he does not know, because of his lack of experience, what the next step should be, and in this free creative work this is the function of the adult, just an idea dropped for the child to pick up and use or ignore as he pleases. If this suggestion is not made the child may become bored and frustrated and will lose any further interest, just when he should be going on to real creative work. Obviously with clay the child's clothes and surroundings will need safe guarding, so an overall with long sleeves that covers him completely and a plastic cloth for him to work on are necessary. The best place for this kind of activity is, of course, the garden.

At all stages, from the first little mound of the two-year-old to the elaborate castles on the sea-shore, sand is a natural and rewarding material to work with. Even in a flat or small house a small amount of sand can be given to a child to play with. An old baby's bath can be made into a container, or a wooden box or even a cardboard dress box can be used. If an adequate covering is put on the floor any spilt sand can be tipped back into the container when the child has finished playing. The playing with sand can be made a progressive activity if the right tools are given to the child to play with as he reaches each stage. At first the child will push it about, making little mounds and holes, and from this find out about the potentialities of sand. Slightly damp sand is easier to use than dry, and a small amount of sand can usually be obtained from a builder if no sea-shore sand is available. As the child develops in creative ability he can be given small jars and pans into which to mould the sand. Wooden spoons are ideal for scooping up the sand, though every now and then the child will find that his hands still make the best tools for his purpose. Small wooden rakes which can be made by a handy mother or father help the child to create all kinds of patterns in the sand. A small large-mesh sieve helps the child to decorate his pies or castles and gives him a new experience when he pours sand through it. Attractive coloured stones and shells are often used by Nursery children to create mosaics in sand or for decoration. A toy motor-car will often stimulate a child to create a series of roads, tunnels and roundabouts, so that here you have the beginnings of learning geography, and incidentally road sense. A group of children made a "river" in the sand, not using water, but simply a channel in the sand, and added to it a fleet of boats they had made on the woodwork table. There are infinite possibilities for the child to use sand in a creative way with a very limited amount of sand in a small container, but he does need, just at the right moment, a suggestion from the adult so that he can extend, widen and deepen his experiences. The suggestion may be a verbal one or simply made by making an addition to the implements in the sand, but without it the child will have exhausted the possible ways of using it from his own inventiveness and become bored and frustrated and then become aggressive, throwing the sand about in a random, wild way. This is always a sign that he needs further encouragement.

As the child comes on to the five-year-old stage he becomes more ambitious and also acquires greater manipulative skills. As he sees his mother sewing, so he wants to sew. This entails more help from the adult, but if he is given a large needle with a double thread and a piece of fairly thick cloth he will take large stitches in it which will turn into a mat for the doll's house or a skirt or a frock for a doll, or even more exciting, a mat for his mother to put the teapot on. He can make a very simple puppet by using a paper bag on which he paints a face, stuff it with anything suitable and tie it on to a cardboard cylinder from a toilet roll. He can then sew a dress on to this. Alternatively, he can simply tie a dress on to the head he has made from the paper bag. He can manipulate this by putting his hand up inside the dress and a finger through the neck of the head. Children find great delight in these puppets and all kinds of phantasy and dramatic play are built up around them. The interest in them may not last very long, but they give much greater pleasure than the specific puppet bought from a shop, and new puppets can be made at no cost when the interest revives again. Incidentally, this is a very useful and engrossing occupation for a child who is confined to bed for any reason.

Bricks of all kinds are useful to the child in his creative play. It is obviously difficult in an ordinary home to allow the child to have many large bricks, such as one finds in a Nursery School, but an inventive child will create all kinds of buildings using boxes and cartons of all sizes and shapes, from the large cereal cartons to egg boxes. They do not last as long as wooden bricks, but they are easily replaceable. A child will play with these for long periods of time and will create imaginatively houses, ships, buses, etc., with which he will play even alone and better still with a companion. There are many kinds of fitting and matching bricks which can now be bought from good toy shops, and which have a more limited and specific purpose, but are at the same time valuable, although they do not allow the same scope for imaginative play. They do help the child with his development of hand–eye co-ordination and finger manipulation and though he does not put them together according to the instructions he will get them together to his satis-faction. Some are definitely too difficult for the child under five, but some are suitable for this free experimenting stage.

Doll play is as important to the child as creative play, and in one way it could be called creative play, since the child will create all kinds of imaginary situations in relation to his doll. A doll may be anything from a rolled up piece of flannel or towelling to an elaborate model dressed in the height of fashion. A great many children find satisfaction in having a piece of material rolled up which really belongs to them. They cuddle it and take it to bed with them and often carry it round while they are playing at something else. It is their constant companion. They have complete power over it and it can be anything they please. It can be their very own baby in imitation, or in rivalry of their mother's new baby. They can ill-treat it in the way they would like to treat the new baby and still know that such behaviour is acceptable to the adults. If a child is emotionally disturbed, if he feels unwanted or rejected, or if his strong aggressive feelings get too strong for him and frighten him, the mere physical contact with his doll will give him comfort and a feeling of security again, particularly if his mother talks to him and enjoys with him his play with his doll. Not all dolls need be as unspecific as the piece of rolled cloth, but the very young child by his choice of this type of material shows us that the less specific kind of doll is the right one for this age. The very elaborately dressed doll which must be carefully treated and looked after is very much enjoyed by the child of about six, but the younger child likes to use his doll for a great many purposes and it has to share in all his activities. The essentials then for a doll for a child of this age are as follows. First, it should be unbreakable. It will have to stand up to a good deal of rough usage, being often used as a scapegoat on to which the child's anger may be directed, or being casually dropped on the floor or in the sand when the child's attention is suddenly directed to something new. Secondly, it must be washable, since the child will take it to share in all his activities . . . and also by bathing his doll the child is imitating his mother and so clarifying feelings and activities to himself. Thirdly, the doll should not, I think, be grotesque or a caricature of a human figure. Unless it is quite unrelated to the human figure, like the piece of material or a teddy bear or a dog, it should have a similarity to a normal human being. A child is likely to be more frightened than amused by a caricature of humanity. Its clothing must be loose and easily fastened or unfastened by a young child. He needs to be independent of adult help when playing with his doll, since the distraction from his play to ask for help will detract from the value of that play.

It is most important that the child should be allowed to use the doll as he likes without interference. The adult often feels that it is wrong to let a child mishandle a doll, beat it and throw it about, but the child in giving to the doll much more severe punishment than he would ever suffer from an adult is getting rid of his feelings of guilt for a real or imagined crime he himself has committed. His treatment of his doll, like his feelings, is ambivalent. He swings very rapidly from harsh treatment to fondling and loving the doll. The doll has been punished and so can be loved again just as he himself wishes to be. In the earlier years the child is quite content to wrap the doll simply in a piece of cloth, but as he gets older he likes to be able to change its clothes, to put it into a nightgown to go to bed or to put on hat and coat to go out in. He likes to relive all the things adults make him do in the person of the doll and so come to a clearer understanding of them. Many children of this age prefer a teddy bear to a doll to play with, perhaps, because, since the teddy bear has no likeness to a human being, the child will have no fears or anxieties about how he treats it.

Certain adjuncts are necessary for fully satisfactory doll play, but at this age not many. A cot or bed is most important, but it can be of the simplest character. A box with a cushion and blanket is perfectly satisfactory. The child simply wants to put the doll to bed, and any kind of receptacle with any kind of covers will do. About five the child will begin to enjoy using a proper cot with proper sheets and pillows and blankets. He plays more objectively and enjoys the reality of life in miniature. A doll's pram is also valuable, and here again any receptacle on four wheels which can be pushed round the floor will serve the purpose. The elaborate expensive doll's pram is a mistake at this age. The child wants something that he can turn to any use which he needs at any given moment. So the doll's pram may become a coal-cart, or be used to carry bricks to a building, or be used as an ice-cream van, according to the child's need, and the specific nature of the elaborate doll's pram prevents him enjoying it in this way. This can be bought for him later when he will really enjoy it. It is essential to remember that doll play is as necessary for boys as it is for girls. Unless they are laughed out of it, they will enjoy just as much the bathing of the doll, putting it to bed and so on, and they, as much as girls, need the clarification and understanding that this play brings. They may through it come to some slight understanding of the role of the father in the family circle and his relationship to themselves.

For the next type of play a different kind of provision is needed. Up to now I have stressed the importance of unspecific play materials, that is materials that can be used in many different ways and are not closely tied up to one particular object or experience. For what is known as world play, however, materials do need to be specific and like the object they are supposed to represent. In world play the child plays with things that resemble, as accurately as possible, things that he meets with in real life. In playing with these objects, he moves them about as he will, he puts them where he wants them, he organises them into groups and relationships, and through these experiences in a microcosm he comes to a better understanding of the real world. Through that understanding he comes to lose some of his fears, his misapprehensions, and his emotional stresses and tensions in relation to the real world and the real objects and people in that world. A doll's house is a good example of the equipment that should be provided. This again need not be an expensive, shop-made article. A box divided into an up and down storey and two rooms partitioned on each floor will give the child the necessary kitchen and sitting-room, bedroom and bathroom. Furniture can be made from matchboxes and small cartons, and because it is home-made can be made in the right size and the correct relationships of one thing to another. The child will need the ordinary furnishings of a house such as he lives in, tables and chairs, television set, kitchen furnishings of gas stove or electric cooker, cupboards, etc., and the same in bedroom and bathroom.

The child will need people to live in his house, and as it is often difficult to get them of the right size, they can be made from pipe-cleaners, cut to size and dressed for father, mother, child and baby. A child will spend endless time moving the furniture round. He may mix it all up and then put it all right again. He puts the things most important in the front, or in the most important room, and then begins to work out categories for the contents of the house. He makes his people in the house behave either as people do behave or as he would like them to behave, and so finds greater clarification of the real world. His power over this miniature world helps him to get rid of his feelings of the inferiority he experiences as a very small child in a very large adult world. The adult can help to give the child the full value of the experience by talking to him and putting the experiences into words and getting the child, if he wants to, to talk about them himself, but there are occasions when if the child is suffering from emotional disturbances, he is better left to work them out for himself, with the sure knowledge that the adult is there to help or reassure at any time. At the same time the adult, by watching the child carefully, may be able to find out what he is thinking or feeling.

All kinds of transport vehicles also provide the child with experiences in world play. These are the things he has seen in the street and around his home and have meaning for him. One feels it is better not to give these very young children plastic cars as they break very easily and can be dangerous. I have seen a small two-year-old bite a piece out of a plastic toy. She was prevented in time from hurting herself, but it could have been serious. Metal cars, lorries and engines are not too expensive and will last a long time for children of different ages for different experiences. Toy Belisha beacons, road signs and traffic lights also give the child many and varied opportunities to experience in miniature what he has seen when out with his mother and father. Besides clarifying these experiences for him they bring the outside world into relationship with his own home and so extend his understanding of associations between his own home and the outside world.

Further experiences in world play can come from the provision of a miniature farm. This could be bought for a Christmas or birthday present. They usually have all kinds of animals, and present in three dimensions what the child, up to now, has probably only known from picture books. Quite often these farm sets include fences, hedges, trees, barns, etc., so that the child will be able to organise his animals into their different categories and put them into different fields or barns. The farm can be added to from time to time, so that always the child keeps his interest and extends his knowledge. For a town child this provides a valuable extension to the knowledge of his environment. Children are naturally interested in animals and the mother or teacher can supply the necessary language, naming the animals and talking about them and extending further by telling the child stories and poems about the countryside. One must, however, try to help the child to understand that just as a real motor-car is bigger than his toy ones, so real animals are much bigger than those he has on his farm; otherwise he may be frightened by the size of real farm animals when he first sees them. All the time, in this world play, one of the adult's jobs is to help the child to realise relative size and distance, though he will probably not come to an appreciation of these differences during the pre-school period.

Another kind of world play which is intensely important to the child is what we might call experiences in scientific enquiry. A child is naturally inquisitive and he will try to find out about the world on his own if we do not provide suitable opportunities for him to do so. This almost invariably results in the child getting into trouble, because his own efforts at finding out how things work so often result in damage, breakages or mess. Therefore, we must give him a variety of objects which he can take to pieces and try to put together again with full adult approval. The question is often asked as to whether if a child is *given* things to take apart and the activity is approved of by the adult, will he not be encouraged to take other things apart which are not approved of? The answer to this is that if the child is given free scope in his play to explore, the need will be satisfied and he will be contented with what he has been given. Four to five years old is usually the time when the inquisitive period begins to be really operative, when the child really wants to know about things. Many things from the ordinary household can be provided from which the child can begin to learn how things work. An old clock, past repair, instead of being thrown out for the dustman, can be given to the child, either as a whole, or taken to pieces so that he can experiment with the springs, etc. He can experiment with turning the hands round and so become interested in the symbols of time progression. If one's nerves can stand it, he can experiment with the bell on an alarm clock, trying to find out how it works. He can be given an old electric torch and find out for himself how to take out and put in the battery. When he has mastered this skill one could give him a live battery to put in so that he can really make light, through his own efforts. The child can be given a bowl of water and various objects, some of which float and some sink, while others sink only gradually. He can be given a magnet and different objects, some of which can be picked up and some not. Fathers come very much into the picture over this scientific learning. He can supply the running commentary ; can explain things as they go along and put into words the child's experiences for him. Also, apart from the child's own exploration, he and the child can do things together. A child is delighted to " help " his father to clean and oil a bicycle or work on the car. He will ask endless questions which all provide the basis for all scientific learning.

Closely allied to the child's scientific learning is his learning about natural history. The pre-school child is at a primitive stage in his development and therefore the primitive in nature has a great appeal for him. Nothing is too simple or too obvious for him to learn about and one must give him every opportunity at this early stage to become familiar with and to have the right attitude towards all growing and living things. Where there is a garden, it is obviously easier to give the child the experiences he needs. The very young baby lying in his pram under a tree, watching the branches move in the wind, the birds flying and the clouds moving, is beginning his education in natural history. As he crawls round on the grass, he feels everything with his hands ; he smells and hears and his sensory perceptions become more acute. As he gets older he becomes interested in how flowers grow ; he can help his father or mother to dig, to plant seeds, to water them and watch all the processes of growth. He may be given a piece of ground of his own in which he can dig and plant seeds and pull them up at intervals to see how they are getting on. He is fascinated by the living creatures in the garden. He shows no fear of nor repugnance for worms or spiders or insects. He will pick them up confidently and expect the adult to share his interest and admiration. We, whatever our attitude may be, must try to share his interest and appreciation, trying not to show our dislike, if any, of spiders and snails and woodlice. We must remember that the child at this stage very quickly senses our reactions, and we may destroy his natural interest and feelings of protection to things smaller than himself, and foster that other primitive impulse to hurt and kill what is smaller and defenceless. So we must try to answer all his questions without showing any emotion. If we don't know the answer, it is a good opportunity to share with the child his first experience of finding information in books.

Even if there is no garden there are many experiences we can give the child in natural history. Many more people these days grow indoor plants and the child can help to look after them. There are other experiences we can give him, such as cutting the tops off carrots and beetroots, putting them in a saucer of water where the child can watch leaves sprout. Beans put into a jam-jar with damp blotting paper will throw out roots and shoots, and mustard and cress planted in a saucer on damp flannel or blotting paper will grow successfully. Planting bulbs in fibre or in a glass jar with water when the formation of roots can be seen is good in winter when there is little else growing to observe. A visit to a pond in the spring can produce for the child one or two tadpoles with water weed in a jar and later other water creatures can be collected in the same way. Even the smallest flat has room for a small aquarium and if the adult knows nothing about it, here again is a chance for the father and mother and child to learn and experiment together. On a visit to a common or a piece of waste land the child can be shown how to pick the ordinary wild flowers, like daisies or buttercups, which are not ordinary or common to him, and he can be shown how to arrange them in a small jar or vase. In the same way trips or holidays to the sea or country can all be used to help him to develop his interests further. But here again, as in all his play and learning, he needs the stimulus of adult suggestion and extension to his own primary interest. Having found out one thing, one fact, he will tend to be quite satisfied, thinking that that is all there is to know, and it is the adult's job to show him that there is more to find out about and enjoy.

The adult must also remember that all this to the child is play and well as work. It is from the play situation that the learning situation develops ; only in this way will the learning be wholly satisfactory. Again we must always keep in mind that the child's learning at this stage must always be practical and objective. He cannot yet deal with abstract deductions, ideas or symbols. He is just beginning to organise his mental concepts and learn how to manipulate them, but this is still to him a very difficult process and on average he will not have much success before the age of six. All the practical investigation that he carries out in his play will lead him on to this later stage of development, and always he must be given the practical observation linked to its appropriate verbalisation with the accompaniment of looking at pictures in books so that one has two types of symbolic representation accompanying the sensory perceptions. All this can be accomplished through play.

CHAPTER 6

Nursery School education. Brief historical survey. Function of Nursery Schools today. Provisions of Nursery Schools to meet the needs of the young child.

THE whole concept of Nursery School education has changed during the last forty-odd years. When the Free Kindergartens and Nursery Schools were set up just at the end of the last century and the beginning of this, the aim was mainly to make up for the physical deprivation suffered by children from bad home situations. Children arriving in our schools at the age of five were often in a shocking physical state. They were suffering from the effects of malnutrition and all the ills that go with it. They had been starved not only of food, but of fresh air and sleep owing to the bad housing conditions. They were dirty and uncared for and had no training in the ordinary decencies of living. Because they had been cooped up in small rooms or had been left with baby-minders who left them in prams or tied to chairs so that they could not get into mischief, they were retarded in muscle control and co-ordination. Their physical abilities were more like those of a very young two- rather than a five-year-old.

The early Nursery Schools concentrated then on the physical side of development. They left the children outside in the open air as far as possible in all weathers. They played outside, ate outside and slept outside for the afternoon rest; they were open-air schools. Most schools made provision for bathing children if they needed it and changing them into clean warm clothes if their

96

own were too dirty, ragged or thin. All of these schools existed on voluntary contributions and therefore there was not much money to spend on food, so it mainly consisted of mince or stew and a milk pudding. Although this diet does not compare with the kind of meals served in Nursery Schools today, it was very much better and more nourishing than anything they got in their own homes. They were all also given milk and cod liver oil. In some cases a small charge was made for the food, but in most cases the parents could not afford to pay anything much. A great deal of time had to be spent in training for social living. Many of the children had had no toilet training ; most of them had to be trained to eat properly. Some were only just weaned before they came to school and had to be taught the whole process of eating solid food. They also had to be taught to wash their hands and faces and comb their hair. Many of the schools provided toothbrushes in order to teach the children dental hygiene. One interesting comment on how the children lived came from a mother who reported that since her child came to the Nursery School she had to have a newspaper spread on the table as a cloth at mealtimes, like they had at school. and that she made the family say " please " and " thank you ". Most of the schools opened at half-past seven in the morning and did not close till five-thirty in order that the mothers who were out at work all day could bring and collect their children and so make a good co-operative relationship with the school.

Most of these schools did a wonderful job of work on the social side, in any kind of building they could get hold of. Many of them were unsuitable in many ways. Many were in old church halls which had only one lavatory and no running hot water. This meant much more work for the teachers, but as long as there was garden space outside and a good play space inside it was possible to carry on satisfactorily, and there is no doubt that under this regime children, even the very young ones, did develop an independence in managing their own affairs, helping the teacher in all the Nursery School routine, feeling very grown up and getting great satisfaction from doing so.

The Fisher Education Act of 1918 changed the outlook on

Nursery education. Teachers in reception classes in the Infant School had reported on how much better in health, how much more independent and developed in every way children who had attended Nursery Schools were on the whole than those who had no such education, and the government began to realise the importance of education in the early years. The Freudian school of psychology which had published its research into the importance of the very early years on later development, particularly in relation to emotional and social development, began to have its findings given wider publicity and a greater amount of acceptance, although there was a good deal of reservation of opinion on the part of some authorities. The health authorities were also stressing more and more the importance of a good physical start to life and this also had an effect. The Government, then, by the Fisher Act, gave limited power to local authorities to give some support to Nursery Schools. They were empowered to grant financial aid to existing voluntary Nursery Schools and where they thought it necessary to set up Nursery Schools of their own or provide facilities for Nursery classes for children under five in their Infant Schools. However, with the approaching recession and the recession itself, very little money was available for such provision and there was very little response, and it was not until the middle thirties that much was done to provide these facilities.

From 1939 to 1945 the needs of the country for women workers in the factories forced the government to make provision for their young children during working hours, and many " Wartime Nurseries " were set up in different parts of the country. These were run concurrently by the Ministry of Health and the Board of Education since they took children under two years old, who were not the responsibility of the Board of Education, as well as children of Nursery School age. This situation was not always easy since a nurse-trained matron was in charge of the whole nursery and a trained teacher in charge of the two- to five-year-olds, and their ideas and attitudes did not always coincide. In the best of these it proved a very successful operation.

After the war some of the buildings were taken over by the Ministry of Health for Day Nurseries, while others were used as Nursery Schools. Another interesting result of the war years also came from the fact that many children were evacuated from bombed centres into residential nurseries and a good deal of research went on into the effects of such evacuation, and the effects of living in groups away from their mothers. This gave acceleration to research into the whole life of the very young child and the results of such an unnatural way of life on their later development. There has been an increase in the number of Nursery Schools since the war, but there are still long waiting lists for each Nursery School and at the moment only about one child in a hundred in an age group has the chance of going to a Nursery School.

An interesting departure from the accepted pattern of school attendance came from the introduction of part-time Nursery Schools by some Local Authorities. Under this plan one group of children attends the school for about three hours in the morning. Then there is a complete break for the staff of about an hour and a half and then a different group of children come for about the same period of time in the afternoon. In some schools one group stays all day and another is only part-time. One feels that the part-time system is a big step forward. The whole day is too long for the young child to be away from his mother. Also it means that the young child is with his mother when those vital important periods of eating and sleeping occur. The child needs the full security of being with his mother when he eats and even more when he goes to sleep. In most cases the children do adjust to the routines of the Nursery School in eating or sleeping, but there are always individual children who have difficulties. Some children definitely have the fear that if they go to bed and to sleep, their mothers may come and go away again without them, and through this fear may force themselves to stay awake however tired they may be. As I have said, it is a very long time for the child to be away from his mother for the first time, and if he lives in a small flat at the top of a high block he may have had very little to do with people outside his own family even in his mother's presence. Suddenly he is thrust into a community of children all of his own age who want the attention of the adult at the same time that he does, and many who may want or have the toys he wants himself. In his naturally egocentric stage he does not see why he should give up anything to another child. The perpetual noise of the Nursery class is bound to be a strain on the child at first and however kind and good the teacher and assistant may be they are both rather unknown quantities. The child does not know what their reactions to his behaviour will be. The usual pattern of this behaviour, although it varies from child to child, is that at first he is very submissive and tentative in his approach to any activity. When he finds that he is encouraged and urged to play with the things he wants, he will swing often quite violently to the other extreme, become aggressive and violent and refuse to co-operate with the adults. He is trying to see how far he can go and how far the adult will protect him and give him security against his own violent feelings and behaviour. He must be able to know that the adult is strong enough and dominant enough to protect him against himself.

From this aggressive type of behaviour, if he is given the necessary support and protection, without punishment or scolding, he will quickly move to the last stage of happy co-operation with adults and other children. Naturally and inevitably he will have lapses from this good behaviour and have difficult periods or days, but the times between such lapses gradually get longer and longer. In order to make the adjustment to the new situation easier for the child, it is a common practice to have the child introduced very gradually. At first his mother comes with him for an hour or so, and then takes him home. Then the time may be extended to two hours. Then the mother may slip away and leave him alone in the nursery for a short time, and so it continues until the child is ready to spend the whole time in school without his mother. Naturally the time it takes for a child to settle in varies from one child to another, and any one child who appears to have settled in very quickly may have a relapse.

Another way in which children are helped is that usually the whole class is not admitted at the same time so that only two or three new children are taken in in any one week until the numbers in the class are complete. New children tend to upset other new children and even children who have been there some time, as one child's distress will communicate itself to others. One problem of the gradual entry system is that of the mother who goes out to work and is unable to accompany her child. In cases like this an aunt or neighbour who has already been looking after the child may act as mother-substitute. Sometimes where two children have been friends at home they may be admitted together and one mother will do duty for both children. In any case, if the part-time Nursery, which is so much better for the child, becomes more prevalent, employers at factories and shops will have to reconsider their employment policy and provide more part-time work for women, which one would think more desirable in any case for mothers with young children. There is still the problem of the widow and the mother of the illegitimate child who has to earn enough to support herself and her family, but special provision might be made for her.

From all the evidence I have heard it does seem that nearly all teachers, parents and children who have tried the part-time system do prefer it. Since the Department of Education and Science recognised Nursery Schools as part of the educational system of the country, hours of attendance in school come into the same pattern as those of the Primary School. They no longer stay open for the long hours they used to. There is a headmistress who is a fully trained teacher and she has under her a teacher in charge of a class. There are also assistants who are often trained Nursery nurses, and often students who work in a Nursery School while undergoing their training for the Nursery nurses' diploma. There are usually also cooks who provide the meals and sometimes women who do the laundry of the children's bedding and overalls, etc. As Nursery School teachers are, like all other teachers, in short supply, sometimes a Nursery nurse will be in charge of a class under the headmistress. The children in a Nursery School as in other Primary

Schools pay only for their food. Part-time Nurseries usually give their children milk and biscuits or fruit as they do not have dinner, but the milk is also given in the full-time school. A nurse makes frequent visits to the school to check up on the children's health and each child is seen at least once by a doctor. It is part of the teacher's job in a Nursery School to keep a careful eye on all the children and to refer to the doctor any individual child she is doubtful about.

Many Education Authorities also make provision for pre-school children in Nursery classes attached to Infant Schools. These are not usually as successful as Nursery Schools since, unless the school is a new one and the Nursery classroom specially built for the purpose, there can be great difficulties. In an older building there is very often no possibility of getting straight from the classroom into the open air. The children have to be taken through long corridors out to the Infants' playground, and this can only be allowed at certain times of the day ; first because they cannot share the playground with large numbers of Infant School children and secondly in some Infant Schools complaints are made about the noise the Nursery children make while they are working. Easy individual movement from classroom activities to open air is essential if the child's needs are to be fully met. Again in some schools, even now, toilets are right across the playground and this means that the child, especially if he is new or nervous, has to be accompanied by an adult and so does not learn independence, and to manage his own affairs, and in wet or wintry weather the situation is fraught with difficulties. In some cases the children find it difficult to sleep because this is the time when the Infant and possibly Junior children are out in the playground, naturally making a noise during their dinner hour. However, a good job is often done under very difficult circumstances and the new Nursery classes provide the same full and rich educational opportunities as the Nursery Schools.

Although the regulations allow that children of two to five should come to the Nursery Schools, most schools do not take children under three. It is felt that in most cases they are too young to leave their mothers, and as there is such a long waiting list for all schools, it is better to let the older children have the chance first. In a special case of home difficulties a two-year-old might be admitted. In most schools the age groups are mixed so that brothers and sisters can be together, and also it has been found that the older children do help the younger ones to settle down, who also learn a lot from imitating them.

One of the problems that has not been tackled is that of the child under five who is admitted into the reception class of the Infant School. A number of these children are being admitted as early as four and a half. Here the child has to go into a class of forty infants, in many cases all new entrants and all requiring the attention of one teacher. In many schools there is a welfare worker who helps with the clothing and washing and toilet of the younger ones, but she has many other duties and cannot spend all her time with the reception class. Moreover, in the worst cases these very young children are expected to sit down and learn in a formal manner to read and write and do arithmetic, all at the same time and long before their natural level of development can possibly understand such proceedings. Many of them will learn under pressure parrot-wise, in order to please the teacher. Their capacity to memorise is very good, but they will not understand what they are doing. This means that as the work gets more difficult their confusion will become worse and they may develop antagonistic attitudes to all school learning. Many teachers believe quite sincerely that they are doing the child a service in " getting him on ", not realising that if it is left to the right moment in his maturation he will not only learn more quickly, but will understand what he is doing, and will therefore be ready to go on to the next stage with eagerness and interest. Let us keep the child under five out of the Infant classroom, even although in its material aspects it may approximate to the conditions of a Nursery School. The large numbers of children with one adult are quite unsuitable for the pre-school child.

How then does the Nursery School run? What kind of programme does it have, and what kind of activities are carried on?

As I have said, the whole concept of Nursery education has changed in the last forty years. The Nursery School is no longer a place where children can be dumped while their mothers go out to work, or a place where the deficiencies in a child's physical development, only, are made good. The aim now is to help the child in his all-round development, to *supplement* the home, but not to *substitute* for it. Therefore the Nursery School takes into account his social development; it attempts to help him to control his strong aggressive impulses or to cease to be over-submissive, cowed and frightened. It tries to give him the widest possible range of experiences so that his intellectual ability will develop; it attempts to surround him with as much beauty both natural and man-made as possible, so that he may develop aesthetically and spiritually, and it attempts to help him to develop physically as fully as possible.

If we look at a day in the Nursery School we may see how the teacher tries to carry this out.

The teacher tries to arrive a short time before the children so that she can put out attractive individual occupations for them to which they can go as soon as they arrive. Things must be ready, as even an old hand may feel a little diffident on the change over of authority and environment fiom home to school and afraid to ask for what he wants until he has settled in. Children arrive gradually in twos and threes, usually with their mothers but sometimes with older brothers and sisters on their way to their own schools. The mother comes into school with the child, helps him off with hat and coat, helps him change shoes and put on an overall if it is provided. She will then usually come right into the classroom with him and see him started on some activity before she leaves him so that there is a carry over from home to school and the break is not too sudden. If the child has had any difficulty either at home or at school she may discuss this with the teacher and together they may find the solution. The headmistress is also at hand in case the mother wants to consult her. It is very much a case of sharing the responsibility for the child. Mothers in this happy free atmosphere will talk to one another and quite often find that they have the same problems and so do not feel that they have a particularly difficult or awkward child. Mothers always seem most generous in admiring one another's children or sympathising with one who has a particular difficulty, and this all makes for a good atmosphere in the school. Moreover (and most important) the friendliness is sensed by the children who therefore feel that other adults are friendly people and to be trusted, and so they get a good impression from what may be their first contact with the outside world.

To establish further the important home–school relationship, many schools run a parent–teacher association. There are meetings for the parents at intervals during the year when the parents can discuss with the staff the children's progress and difficulties, and in these discussions the parents help the staff as much as the staff help the parents. Sometimes there are lectures or discussions with a visitor who is a specialist on one or on all sides of child development. Sometimes films of children or educational institutions are shown. Sometimes there is a purely social evening with refreshments and perhaps dancing. Sometimes jumble sales are held at which the parents help, in order, as well as providing cheap goods to the customers, to raise money for extra equipment which cannot be supplied by the Education Authority. All the teachers feel that it is important that the fathers take part in these functions as well as the mothers so that the whole family is involved in the home–school relationship. It is by such means that the parents come to consider that the school is theirs as well as the children's— and after all, they are paying for it !

The teacher, as I have said, will have arranged her room beforehand. She will change certain play materials from day to day, but she will always provide for the different kinds of play that are necessary for the child and the individual needs of different children according to their developmental level. There are certain play materials which are basic, which will be used by all children at

different times in different ways. One of the most important of
these is the Wendy house or home corner, which may become in
turn a hospital corner or a hairdressing salon or a hiding place for
burglars, according to the children's particular interests at any
given time. The Wendy house may vary from an elaborate wooden
structure with windows and a door to a wooden clothes-horse
covered with material and fastened to the wall at one side so that
it does not fall over. The furniture within the house can be added
to or taken away from as the teacher wants to stimulate or extend
interests, but there is certain basic equipment which one would
always have there. A bed with a cover, where mother or baby or
patient can lie, is most important. A wooden box which can be
used as cooking stove, or electric cooker or even a television set is
needed. Some cups and saucers and a saucepan provide for the
important phantasy meal times, most important for a child who is
having food difficulties. A table and two chairs are also useful.
Dolls should also be there ready for use by one or more children.
Other things will be brought into the house by the children themselves as they need them, but it is wiser not to put in too much at
first as a cluttered house will only cause frustration and aggression.
The children themselves will take other things from the Nursery
as they require them for the special games they are playing.

Near to the Wendy house and hanging up so that they can easily
be distinguished should be the dressing-up clothes, which will
further stimulate dramatic and phantasy play. Here would be the
nurse's apron and cap, all kinds of old hats which can be put to any
number of plays by the inventive child; old felt hats are particularly
useful as they can be pummelled into any shape for cowboys,
firemen, policemen, etc. Indian headdresses can be easily made
with curtain tape and feathers collected by staff or children. A
cloak with elastic in the neck so that it easily slips over the head
can be used in endless ways, and long skirts, again with elastic, so
that they fit all figures, are used by both boys and girls in all sorts
of ways. Old adult shoes and handbags provide the authentic
reality touch to the " mother " or " lady ". These unspecifi-

garments are essential as the children can adapt them to their particular needs, but the teacher can supply more specific garments like a piece of net for a bridal veil. As the children's plays develop, the teacher will produce the right equipment, following the children's lead. She will also watch the children's television programmes so that she can provide the clothes suitable for the heroes of the films that the children are seeing, or she can provide clothes suitable for the characters of the stories she has told them, like *Little Black Sambo's Umbrella.*

The Wendy house, then, is a vital piece of equipment for in it the children find the security of playing out difficulties in the home, of playing out situations which need clarification and understanding. It helps their social development and shows them in miniature the different hierarchies in society. One child is a leader and one is the led ; one child is demanding and aggressive while one is giving and submissive ; one child will come to the rescue of a weaker one against a stronger, and already for a few minutes one may find a small group " ganging-up " against one child who is unpopular. The patterns of social living are beginning to appear and it is the teacher's job now and again to interfere and restore harmony where things have gone wrong. Where the Junior School children sort out their own difficulties the Nursery School children are still dependent on the adult to show them the right attitudes and behaviour towards other children and to protect them against their own impulses of strong aggression and egocentricity. The teacher, however, must interfere as a person in her own right in the world of reality and not as part of the phantasy play. In the child's mind at this stage there is confusion between phantasy and reality. Because of his complete identification with the character he is playing his phantasy is as real to him as the real world, therefore he needs the protection of the adult in the real world to help him to overcome the difficulties of the phantasy world. As I said before, he feels in complete control of the phantasy situation ; he is the powerful figure in command and he will lose his sense of security in the adult if he feels he can make her do whatever he likes, whereas in the real world the adult is the person in power who can do no wrong. One does see frequently students and young teachers entering too emphatically into the phantasy play of children and so causing them confusion and insecurity.

As the Wendy house is essential, so are bricks for building. I have already mentioned them in relation to the home situation, but in the Nursery School the scope for using them is obviously much greater. The hollow wooden bricks seem most suitable as they are light and easy to handle and will not cause much damage if thrown in a moment of aggression. They come in varied sizes and the teacher can add to them lengths of wood and pieces of wood in different shapes, arches, wheels, etc. These stimulate the children's imagination and give them ideas which are not directly imposed by the teacher. The bricks should be placed near to a wall so that they can be propped against it, and a good clear space is necessary so that the building can extend out into the room without the danger of people tripping over it and knocking it down. Children will play individually or in small groups with the bricks. At first they will have great delight in building towers and knocking them down, but when this type of play becomes over-excited and wild, so that the children might get hurt, then is the time for the teacher to step in and drop a suggestion for a new form of play. Because of her good relationship with the children this suggestion is usually accepted and the children go on to develop it in their own way. This may be something quite different from the first suggestion, but they needed it just to start them off. Playing with bricks helps with the development of manipulative dexterity and control ; it helps with social development in the exchange of ideas ; it helps with the formation of concepts of space, of length, of height and breadth; it helps to make imaginative phantasy become reality. Finally it helps the child in learning to control his emotions as he gets rid of his violently aggressive feelings by being destructive in knocking down buildings and then turning his destructive energy into constructive channels by building them up again. Bricks present him with a challenge which he meets and conquers at his own level.

The " plastic " materials are of great importance. Materials that can be banged and pummelled, moved about and shaped as the child pleases. These are materials which he can manipulate in any way he pleases and which can present an even greater challenge as he becomes more skilled and practised in the use of them. Some of these the teacher will always have available for the children ; others she may change from day to day. Sand is one which should always be there, and in the Nursery School one can go far beyond the scope of the provision made for the child in the home without a garden, where it must be limited to a small box or tray. There will be a large tray in the classroom for use in wet weather or for children who are not yet secure enough in the environment to leave the classroom, but the main work in sand will be in a sand pit in the garden, which should be large enough to hold at least ten children. Here there should be made available both damp and dry sand, wet sand for moulding and dry sand for pouring and sieving or simply running through the fingers for the feel of it. Tools for the sand should include wooden spades and spoons (never metal ones), pails and bun tins for making pies, wooden rakes, sieves and plastic bottles and, as the need arises, the teacher can add equipment to promote or extend any play begun by the children. Thus one or two tin soldiers encourage the building of castles and forts ; one or two boats may encourage the formation of rivers and so on. There are endless ways of helping the children to extend their experiences and form new mental concepts by the simple introduction of different pieces of equipment. As the interest in one experience flags and comes to an end, so a new one, or one that has been used before and discarded, should be introduced.

Water play comes under this category and is most valuable. The children can do with it what they please and yet it reacts in surprising and exciting ways, so that there is always much for the children to learn. There are many variations in water play which can be introduced to the children, but the one always available for the children should be a water tray large enough for four children to play at a time without getting in one another's way. The tools in the water tray should all be unbreakable and not too many at a time. It is better to have a few at a time and ring the changes on them rather than so clutter up the tray that the child cannot get at the water. There will be needed in the tray containers that differ in size so that one small one can fill a bigger one ; this is the beginning of learning about capacity. Then the child will want to know how water behaves in different circumstances, so he will need a funnel, a sieve, a bottle that squeezes and a rubber tube. These are basic for general experience of water, at other times different materials can be put in instead, like boats made from different materials such as wood, cork, plastic and paper, and a boat made from foam-rubber gives the children the experience of seeing how long it takes for it to sink. A change again can be made to a variety of articles, some of which float and some that sink. The child thus learns about the properties of water in relation to the properties of other materials and as we have seen, it is most important for him, for his intellectual development, to be able to form mental relationships. Variations on the basic water play can be introduced one at a time, although the water itself is always available.

These would include such activities as bathing the dolls, washing the dolls' clothes and blowing bubbles. With all of these, however, there is a certain amount of skilled technique involved and the child will need the adult's help and supervision. For instance, in washing the dolls' clothes the child must be shown how to wash them in soapy water, how to rinse them in clean water and how to hang them out to dry. Because she has seen her mother do these things she will want to do them properly ; she has not learned how to do them until she has tried, but will be frustrated if the result is not good, like her mother's, and she must have the adult to help her beyond the experimenting stage. Bubble-blowing is also quite a difficult skill. It involves quite a lot of breath control and hand control to achieve a good result, and usually it is too difficult for the child under four, so that one would not encourage a child under that age to try this experience. For those of four years old who do succeed, it gives a great feeling of creative power and delight.

I have already mentioned clay as an important medium for the children to use, but in the Nursery School there is more scope for larger amounts of clay to be used and the interaction of one child on another in experimenting and creating with clay. On a plastic cloth the child can push the clay around as he likes and the teacher must remember that hands are the right instruments for early work with clay. So often the children are given cutters and rollers to use with clay right from the beginning and so form a dislike of handling it. Yet it is a primitive material to be used by hands in this primitive stage of development. The teacher must be careful that the clay is kept in good condition, never allowed to become hard so that it is completely frustrating, and yet not so wet and sloppy that it cannot be moulded properly. The children must have a long time of experimentation, finding out about the qualities of clay before they are ready to make something with it. It is only when the child begins to get wildly aggressive with it and obviously showing signs of boredom that the teacher might drop a suggestion about making things.

I think it is undesirable for the teacher to make things herself for the child, as he cannot possibly reach her adult standard of performance and hence may give up trying on his own level. If, however, the children show reluctance to play with clay because it is " dirty ", the teacher could encourage them by sitting down with them and simply rolling the clay in her hands without making anything. The important thing for the teacher to remember is that she must not *expect* an end product. That the experimenting with clay is the learning process going on and has an intrinsic value of its own. If by chance a child does make something and gives it a name, it means that he has reached a new stage of development for which he is ready, but he must not be pushed on to that stage or he will not get the full value from it. Teachers often find it difficult to accept the fact of the educational value of experimenting with materials without producing a concrete result. This is, of course, due to our own early conditioning and training. We still cannot accept the fact that the young child in his play knows what he can do, his limitations, and what is right for him at any stage.

Facilities for painting should also always be available for the children. Easels with paper ready on them, with jars of paint and a brush for each jar, should be placed wherever possible where they are out of the way of children coming and going. Powder paint should be so mixed that it gives a good strong colour. Thin wishy-washy colours have little value. They cannot express what the child wants to express. Usually three or four colours are enough and they should be changed from day to day so that the children widen their experiences. Paper can be cut in different shapes as well as the rectangular, in order to stimulate the children's concepts of shape and size, and should be of different textures and colours. These give a wide variety of experiences and some children achieve beautiful pattern effects when painting on triangular or circular paper. The child's need in painting, besides exploring the possibilities of paint and paper, is to express himself and to communicate those feelings which he cannot yet put into language. Therefore the teacher's job is to see that he can do this immediately when he feels the need. If he has to go and hunt for paint or paper or wait while it is got ready for him, his first eager impulse to paint will be frustrated and he may lose interest altogether in creative work of this sort. The teacher can also help the child by suggesting that he paints. Sometimes it does not even occur to him that he could paint, and in other cases he is too shy and withdrawn to make the first attempt. The teacher can also help the child by talking to him about his painting, not necessarily asking him what it is, because a child of this age usually paints first and names it afterwards. Often to adult eyes the name seems to have little relation to the shapes he has painted, but one takes his word for it and admires it. The real involvement and interest of the teacher in the child's work will stimulate and encourage him more than anything else.

Another important item in the classroom, and one that is always there, is the book corner. Here again the books must be easily available for the children to take whenever they want. A stand with pockets in it, so that the books stand upright and are easily seen by the children, is the best method of presentation. Books must be of all kinds and must, of course, contain pictures. These books should as far as possible be related to the children's own experiences both in the classroom and at home. Therefore one would have books about a child's activities at home, helping his mother to sweep and dust, going shopping with her, going on a bus or for a walk, and, very important for those who are suffering from a new baby at home, books about a child helping his mother with a baby; books of nursery rhymes the children have learnt with music as well as pictures and print, and books of the stories the teacher has told them so that the children can " read " them for themselves. Even more important are the books the teacher makes herself that are concerned with the activities in the classroom, for instance, a book of the musical instruments they use, a book of the interest table, a book of birds seen in the nursery garden, a book of the tools used on the woodwork table, and a book of paintings or of paintings done by the children themselves. There are not enough books published that are suitable for children of this age, therefore the teacher must provide some home-made ones herself, trying to show to children, even at this early age, that books are interesting in themselves, quite apart from the interest of the teacher's praise when she sees a child occupied with a book. One wants to create the right incentive for learning to read right from the beginning, and it is always possible, even in the Nursery School, to find a child who has reached the reading-readiness stage. The teacher can further the children's interest in books by sometimes sitting in the book corner with a group of two or three children reading a book to them while they watch her turn the pages, as long as she keeps an eye on the other children.

I have already mentioned the kinds of instruments that can be made for and used by the pre-school child for varied musical experiences and these are a necessity in the Nursery School. They should be added to and changed frequently so that the children are encouraged to carry on with the exploration of sounds. They should always be available for the children unless the teacher needs a reasonably quiet classroom, for instance, when she is telling a story, in which case the needs of the individual child must give way to the needs of the many. It is wise to put musical instruments next to the piano so that the children may be able to relate the experiences to one another easily, and, of course, there will be music books on the piano which may or may not be related by the child to the sounds he is making. Here again the teacher may help the children by sometimes joining them at the music table and playing any of the instruments, or sitting down at the piano and playing an accompaniment to their music or at odd times putting on a gramophone record for them.

This incidental joining in with the children is most valuable, but it always must run concurrently with the child's own undirected experimenting with the musical instruments. As soon as a teacher joins a group, since she is an adult she automatically to some extent directs it and the children must have the free individual self-chosen activity as well for the fullest development. It is, however, useful for the teacher to jot down the free rhythms or tunes that the children make for themselves so that she can gain a fuller understanding of their natural rhythms and feeling for melody. She can then use this understanding in her more directed work in music with them. Sometimes the children can be encouraged to link their music with their other play activities. For instance, in one Nursery School the children were engaging in a lot of Indian play. With the teacher's help they constructed a totem pole and then spontaneously began to dance round it. One bright little boy went and got a drum off the music table, which he beat in time with the dance, and very shortly thereafter every child in the group had an instrument which he played while he danced, producing a very marked natural rhythm. This time it all came from the children, but on another occasion this might come from a suggestion dropped by the teacher for the children to accept or not, as they please. Music should be an integral part of the day's programme, and not just a set period when the children do what the adult directs. On some days if the children are disturbed or aggressive for any reason, music played on a gramophone or on the piano by the teacher will help them to settle down to sleep more easily. One would not do this every day in case one formed the habit of the child never going to sleep without music, which might make things difficult for the mother at home. The teacher should be careful never to play music which she does not enjoy herself. The children will sense very quickly her dislike and will get little value from the experience.

Last, and perhaps most important of the materials that should always be provided for the children's education, is the nature or interest table. It should be an attractive centre-piece to the room, not tucked away into a corner, but well in the middle of a wall so that the children see it as soon as they come into the room. Young children are intensely interested in growing things, so that the first things that are provided must be things that grow whatever the season of the year, and luckily there are always things that do grow. I have already mentioned some of the things that can be provided, like carrot-tops, beans in jars, mustard and cress. But bulbs, also planted in good time, will come up before the Christmas holidays, so that the children get full value from them, and in the spring a miniature garden, planted with grass and seedlings and small plants, wild or cultivated, gives the children great pleasure and education. It is important that the children should be encouraged to help with the nature table, in the planting and watering of seeds and plants, so that they recognise man's part in the growth of plants and feel some responsibility for it.

Besides growing plants there should be vases of leaves and flowers. Small vases can hold both wild and cultivated flowers and small children can be helped to arrange them easily by placing a circle of cardboard with a hole in the middle over the top of the jar or vase ; this supports the flowers easily. It is not too early to show them how to arrange the table with tall vases at the back and short ones in front. Besides making the table more attractive, it also helps them to gain concepts of high and low, tall and small. They should be encouraged to smell the flowers and plants as well as to name the colours and also the flowers. Every flower and leaf, however common to us, is exciting to them.

One would also place on the nature table other objects of interest, like different coloured stones put into a glass bowl with water in it, so that they shine ; shells of all kinds, from sea-shells to snail shells ; feathers from all kinds of birds, a disused bird's nest, seaweed and fruits from trees like acorns and chestnuts. All of these have a fascination for children and the list is endless. Living creatures can be included, such as tadpoles in season, worms in a home-made wormery, goldfish and water creatures in an aquarium. A hamster in a properly constructed box gives to the children the idea of looking after and protecting animals who are active and do things like they do—eat and sleep, for instance. However, one would never let children play with or look after such creatures unsupervised. There should be a constantly changing progression on the nature table according to the season of the year, so that the children's interest is always stimulated by something new and attractive to look at and to ask questions about. Needless to say the teacher must be ready with the answers to such questions, but these answers should be short and factual ; a child of this age cannot take in a great amount of detail, nor generalisations about plant or animal life.

Added to this experience of nature within the classroom should be the experience outside in the garden. Even where a Nursery School or a Nursery Class has only an asphalt playground, use can be made of gardens in tubs or boxes. Where there is a garden, it should supply a constantly changing picture of colour and form in shrubs and flowers, managed by the teacher and children or by the janitor and sometimes by gardeners supplied by the Local Education Authority. Wherever possible there should be a place where the children can dig, plant their own seeds, water them and pull them up at times to see how they are getting on. In this way they can observe the natural growth of roots and shoots. One would choose for this purpose very hardy, quick growing-plants like nasturtiums or marigolds, which will take a lot of hard treatment. The children find enormous satisfaction in watching the progress of growth, and when the flowers appear, in cutting them and arranging them in vases. They feel the triumph of having grown something themselves. Also in the garden I would have a wild patch where wild flowers grow in the grass. Many town children have never seen buttercups and daisies growing naturally, and many wild flowers can be translated easily to the garden for the children. Our aim should be to give the town child as many experiences as are enjoyed by the country child, as possible. A country environment is the right one for any young child.

These then are the basic necessities in any classroom for Nursery children, but the teacher will need to have other materials which she will change from day to day, either when she feels that the children need a further stimulus or because they ask for certain activities which they have had before. For a more easily malleable material than clay she will introduce dough, which, if brightly coloured with powder paint, will be used for modelling and may serve as an introduction to clay for children who find the latter too difficult to use. Children under direction may be helped to make cakes which can then be baked in the school kitchen and eaten at school or taken home. This is a popular activity, but the teacher should not become too involved with too large a group of children doing this at the same time. If they take turns they are learning lessons in social behaviour as well as all the values of doing " cooking " like mother at home.

There are many extensions of painting, most of which I have mentioned already, which the teacher can provide, such as drawing with crayons and large black pencils, using different media to paint with, and using finger paint. Since the teacher has a great many more children to provide for than the mother in the home, it is essential that she should have a wide variety of creative materials in order to meet her children's individual needs, which do not only differ from one another, but change from day to day. Creative work is vital for all children, but how this creative urge is satisfied varies from child to child.

Doll play must also be provided, though participation in this seems to be more sporadic. Sometimes a child or a group of children will play with the doll in a pram or in a Wendy house for a long time with great concentration. At other times such play is completely ignored and the doll's pram is used for a transport wagon or to wheel a real child in. It is interesting to note that a new child in the Nursery will often play with dolls when she will not attempt any other activity, and perhaps all children, when they are feeling slightly insecure, will take to doll play in order to get back their feelings of confidence and security.

Extensions of brick building activities should be provided in the shape of more specific materials. For instance, shaped wood which can be fitted together to make road tracks and bridges, along which the children can run their toy cars, or railway tracks that will fit together. These provide the opportunity for much social play, though quite often the teacher has to step in and help the children when the fitting together is difficult. Again, there are many varieties of fitting together small bricks, made either of wood or plastic materials. The young Nursery child will fit them together haphazardly, but the manipulation helps him with his hand control and whatever kind of object he produces he is proud of it. An even more limited type of construction is provided by wooden articles like cars, lorries, engines and ships, which can be taken apart and put together again by means of wooden screws. This is a difficult operation for the under-five and it is mostly the older children in the Nursery who can attempt it. Because it can produce only one specific object, it has a limited value for Nursery School children.

Fitting toys of different kinds are of value to a child who wants a quiet period of concentration. They are mainly based on the principles of Doctor Montessori's sense training apparatus and provide training in hand–eye co-ordination, finger manipulation and the beginnings of recognition of spatial relations and of recognition of colour, shape and form.

The most popular of such toys are jigsaw puzzles which vary from very easy ones, where the child lifts out a complete figure from a background picture, to a quite difficult and complicated real jigsaw puzzle. It must be remembered that a child of this age doing a puzzle will fit the pieces together, not from a recognition of colour or part of an object, but from the actual shape of the piece. Therefore if the teacher is making a jigsaw puzzle of her own or choosing them for her class, she must be sure that each piece is of a different shape, so that when the child has finished the puzzle he will recognise the picture he has made. Another activity children enjoy is threading beads. These should be large wooden beads and the best kind of string to use is a boot-lace with a metal tag at the end which pushes easily through the beads. Other activities which give the child the same kind of satisfaction and education are inset boards with geometrical shapes, peg boards where the child makes his own patterns of colour and line, mosaics of different descriptions, a posting-box and nesting cubes. Many variations of this material can be made by the teacher herself.

Other variations on manipulative materials which I have already mentioned are sewing and sticking and cutting. These are really only suitable for the older children in the Nursery and do need a good deal of supervision and help from the teacher and one would not expect much in the way of results from the children. They are learning skills and techniques which they will later use for the achievement of an end product. In providing materials for pre-school children, one must always take into account these two aspects : media which provide the child with the opportunity to experiment, to manipulate, to create freely and independently at his own level, and media which, with adult help, provide him with the opportunity to develop skills and techniques which will be of use to him later in school. Most materials provide both these opportunities, but some are designed more for one aspect than for the other.

As the child sees his mother cleaning at home and may have helped her, so he likes cleaning at school. These cleaning jobs can take in the whole range of what his mother may do at home, from sweeping and dusting. Other occupations which may be offered to him are cleaning out cupboards and tidying them; polishing tables and chairs; cleaning shoes; cleaning the silver used at dinner, and helping the assistant to wash up cups used for milk. All of these activities need a good deal of help and supervision from the adult, and a good standard of work should be required from the child. This will probably mean that the teacher has to finish off the job for him in order that he should see that the required standard is reached.

Materials which provide for big muscular movement and all the development of the bigger muscular skills are usually provided by the Local Authority and the teacher may not have much say in the matter, but she may in many cases suggest what apparatus she would like. A jungle gym is an essential, since it provides the children with many experiences, not only physical, as a great deal of imaginative and social play will develop from the use of it. Children develop great confidence as they go on using it freely and in their own way; it is almost unknown for a child to fall or hurt himself while playing on this piece of apparatus, but he must never be pressed beyond his own wishes. If he is allowed to develop his skills gradually in his own time, he will never be afraid of falling and therefore will not fall. The teacher may drop a suggestion to help him to extend his experiences, but must be ready to have that suggestion ignored if the child feels that he is not yet ready to act upon it.

In the same way a slide, not too high and with raised sides, is safe and gives endless opportunities for development of skills. It also leads to the natural taking of turns, a valuable art to be learned at this stage if the child is ready. Climbing ropes and nets are also seen in many Nursery Schools, but are rather difficult for that age to cope with. They might be better if left to a later stage; in the Nursery they are never as much in use as the jungle gym and the slide. Very valuable to children are large boxes and planks and old motor tyres with which they can build up their own climbing frames, houses, ships and buses, and once having built something, and the teacher has inspected it to see it is safe, the children will have endless adventures, experimenting with physical movement as well as imaginative play. Tricycles are much in demand in the Nursery School and the children show much skill in riding and steering them. It is, however, one of the teacher's duties to see that the children get their turns in the right order and that one or two children do not monopolise them. She must always be rigidly fair over this, however much she may be aware that one child needs the experience with the tricycle, needs to have his own way more than the others. This is a case where the individual, however great his need, has to give way to the needs of the greater number of children.

Toys to push and pull are also necessary in the garden. A miniature ox-cart which can be pulled by one or two children with one traveller inside, has great value in social development as well as helping muscle control, while the " two-wheeler " or scooter present a challenge in balancing which the older children are ready to accept and conquer. Smaller apparatus, like bats and balls, bean bags and shuttlecocks, all give the children experiences of running and catching, throwing and hitting accurately, which they enjoy for a short time. Most Nursery Schools provide variations in this equipment, but as long as the children have opportunities for climbing and hanging, for pushing and pulling, for running and walking and balancing freely and for developing further in strengthening and co-ordinating muscles, their needs will be met. The greater the variety there is the better, in order to meet the needs of individual children, but one must be careful not so to fill the garden with apparatus that there is not enough room for the children to run round freely without falling over obstacles.

The teacher will have put out her equipment for the children's free play, and one may expect any one child with long experience of the Nursery to ask for materials which he has used before, and if possible she will supply them for him, but she must also make provision for the children in the shape of adult-directed groups. These group times usually provide for story-telling, language training, natural science experiences and music. At this age not all the children want to do the same thing at the same time, so no Nursery School teacher would make any group activity compulsory for any child. She will have very wide differences among her children of chronological age, of mental and social and emotional development, therefore attendance must be voluntary. Much of the value of the group activity is lost to all the children when the teacher has to spend much of the time insisting that one or two children sit down and listen when they have no desire to do so. No mother would insist that a child of this age must listen to a story if he did not want to, and the teacher should, as far as is possible, follow the good mother's example. She will be aware of the time when the majority of her children have satisfied for the time being their need for independent self-chosen activities, and that they need the security of more adult-directed activity, and she will therefore by clearing some of the apparatus away, but also leaving enough for children who do not want to join in, make a space for her activities. Sometimes the children will express a wish for a certain type of group activity and she will naturally fall in with their wishes, but it is important that within any one day the children should be given the opportunity of listening to a story and participating in some kind of music even if only one or two children join in.

The teacher should keep in mind her aims in telling stories to such young children. Perhaps the most important is that children should learn to enjoy stories and so come to enjoy literature. This means that any story the teacher chooses for her children she must enjoy herself and she must show her enjoyment to the children. A story must always be *told* to a group of children of this age, not read to them. If a teacher has studied a story and assimilated it, it means that she will have added something of herself to the story in re-creating it for her children, and any one story told by different teachers will make a different impact on the children. While telling a story she is able to watch the children, catch their eyes and share her enjoyment with them, but with her head buried in a book she will be unable to do this and half of the enjoyment of it is lost to them. As I have said before, it is a good thing for a teacher to read a story to two or three children in the book corner, but this is a quite different experience for them. The normal story group is too large for this.

Another primary aim in telling stories to children is to extend their language learning. Therefore the language of any story must be good literature. It must contain mainly familiar vocabulary, but new words and phrases must be introduced in a context through which the children can understand them, or the teacher can explain certain words or phrases, which she thinks they will not understand through context, either by simple verbal definition or by showing them an object or a picture. If a new word is vital to the understanding of the story, as, for instance, the turnip in the *Tale of the Turnip*, by Elizabeth Clark, then this would be done before the story begins so that explanations should not interrupt the flow of the story.

As children are at a naturally rhythmic stage in their development, the language of the story should be rhythmical as far as possible. This is well illustrated in well-known folk tales. Further, there should be plenty of repetition, in which the children can join, so that they learn language by repeating it themselves as well as hearing it. The teacher in telling the story must tell it slowly enough for the children to follow, remembering their limited facility in understanding language, but at the same time it must be fast enough to carry the story along and the children with it. A very slow delivery will spoil the rhythm of it. If it is a well-chosen story, the telling of it need not be dramatic; an over-dramatic rendering will come between the drama of the story and the child and will prevent him from assimilating it and forming his own conceptions of it. He must be given the chance to recreate it in his own mind. Some teachers adopt a rather sing-song voice when telling a story to very young children, and this completely destroys the naturalness of the language of the story, which will then be unrelated to the children's and teacher's ordinary use of language. If the language is natural, she will find the children repeating words from the story and relating them to their own play activities. At the end of the story the teacher may, if the children want it, have a short discussion, or summing up, but often the children do not want this interruption of their assimilation and re-creation of the story—in which case it should be just left to develop in its own way.

Through stories also children will be able to extend their mental concepts. Experiences they have had will be put into words for them. They will hear of things that other people do as well as themselves and they will be given the language to explain these sensory percepts and so form mental concepts about them. They may also be helped without realising it to make relationships between concepts, to compare and contrast them and manipulate them in a more mature way. They will hear of all kinds of new experiences, most of which are related to the world in which they themselves are living, but also of others, which could not possibly happen to them. In this way they will gradually come to appreciate the fact that there are two worlds, one a world of reality, like the one in which they live. In this world all kinds of experiences may happen which to us may be ordinary and commonplace, but to a child of this age they are exciting and adventurous. And then there is the other world of phantasy and magic. To the young child these two are very much the same thing. He passes quickly from one to the other without realising it. It is a sign of maturation, when the child can make the division between these two worlds, and it is important that he should do so at the right time. An adult who will retreat into a phantasy world on all occasions in order to escape from the difficulties of the reality world is suffering from mental illness. So we help the child gradually and slowly to achieve the realisation of the dichotomy of worlds when he is ready for it and one of the ways to do so is through telling him stories of both types of world.

Further stories may be used for help in release from emotional fears and tensions. It will help a child to have such feelings as fear, aggression and guilt brought out into the open in relation to another child, not himself, when he will not feel the guilt or embarrassment that he might if one talked to him directly about it. Thus stories about children going to hospital, stories about children whose mothers have new babies, stories about children who have temper tantrums, stories about children who enjoy being in the dark after they have got over their fears about it, can all be helpful. One must let the child be aware that these fears are recognised as being real and understood, but also how they can be conquered by children in the same situation as themselves. This awareness will be unconscious on the part of the child, but it will help him. A child listening to a story that is well told and without interruptions will identify himself with the characters in the story and become involved with them as he does with the characters in his own phantasy play. He cannot look at them and enjoy their adventures objectively, as the older child will do. These adventures happen in his own self-contained autistic world.

The choice and finding of stories for this age is not easy, because there are not many books of suitable stories. One has often to hunt through a whole book of stories to find one suitable, but there are certain basic principles which a teacher will remember when choosing them. First, as we are introducing children to literature, they must be well written in good simple language, with fairly short sentences and plenty of repetition. Occasional rhymes help to carry the story along, and satisfy the child's need for rhythm. In order to hold the children's interest, there must be plenty of action and not too much description, and because one is setting a pattern for stories to them, it must have a beginning, a middle and an end. This means that there must be the introduction of the people *before* they can begin having experiences. Too many stories written for children begin with such sentences as : " Johnny was walking down the garden one day ", or " It was Johnny's birthday ". This is no use to the young child ; one cannot plunge him into the middle of things ; he must know something about Johnny first. There is no better way to start a story than the old traditional one of " Once upon a time there was . . .".

A great many of stories for these children should be placed in situations they themselves know and understand, but one will also give them stories of other situations which will help them to get some idea of the world beyond. However, one must realise that these ideas may not have any real relation to the adult's concepts of such worlds. A group of Nursery children were taken into the country from the East end of London. They had been told stories about farm animals and shown pictures of them, but when they were taken to a farm they were frightened by the size of the animals they saw. Later on they were up on the downs and saw far below them in the fields cows feeding, looking very small at that distance, and one child remarked at once, " Look, there are *real* cows ! " Therefore, when we are giving them concepts of the real world beyond their experience, those concepts will still be at their own level. They like stories then, about real children, about children like themselves, and they also like stories about animals.

Here again, because of their difficulty of differentiating between phantasy and reality, one would rather give them, on the whole, stories about real animals, behaving in the way that they really do. The type of stories where animals behave like human beings, attractive as some of them are, are more suitable for, and are more enjoyed by, older children. One would be careful also not to tell stories that are too frightening. Some of the stories of the Brothers Grimm, for instance, come too close to the primitive savagery of the stage young children are still living in, and may prove emotionally disturbing to any particular child, so that he suffers from nightmares and day-time fears. These are better kept for the stage when the child can enjoy the stirring up of his emotions objectively and so come to terms with it easily.

Again, because of the young child's need of complete security within the family situation, his need to admire and love both father and mother, one would never tell stories in which the parents do not live up to the ideal of parenthood. Tales of wicked fathers and mothers, or wicked stepmothers or stepfathers, who might be in any given child's experience a successful mother or father substitute, should be left to a later stage. At the same time stories in which the bad character is killed do not seem to affect pre-school children. They have no idea what death means. Unless they have actually had a death in the family, their ideas are based on adults' talk, which has little real meaning for them, or on the films they have seen on television, where the " bad " man is killed, but may be seen again the next day in a different film. This is obvious from their play of Cowboys and Indians, when they will fall down " dead " and the next moment be careering round the garden. It is, however, quite impossible to them that a good person should die and we must take account of this in the stories we tell them.

It is obvious from what I have said about the paucity of the right kind of stories for children of pre-school age that the teacher will inevitably have to make up many of her own stories, particularly when she wants to meet the needs of one particular child, or a particular group of children. Only she can supply this kind of story. Luckily, Nursery School children like the safety and familiarity of the same story over and over again. Story-telling time is a most enjoyable one in the Nursery School and not only can the teacher give the children so many educational values from the experience, but she herself can find out more about her children from their reactions to different stories. Story time is therefore essential, but it is also essential that attendance at it should be voluntary, otherwise in very many cases it will defeat its own ends.

The teacher, as I have said, will have given the children many opportunities for experiences with all kinds of making music, both rhythm and melody, but how does one take a " music lesson " with such young children? In the first place, like the story group it must have voluntary attendance. Not every child wants to have a musical experience at the same given moment each day, and if he is made to join in, he will not only gain very little, if anything, but will prove to be a disrupting force to the rest of the group. It is an interesting fact that when a new teacher has taken over a class from a teacher who has insisted on all the children joining in, she finds that when making it voluntary her group dwindles to as little as two or three children, but as the children come to find pleasure and satisfaction in the experiences she gives them, her group will grow again until it totals almost the whole class. There will always be two or three abstainers who are not ready for such a group experience, and will therefore gain nothing from it. I would like to make the point, however, that the teacher should always encourage the children to join in but never press them. Sometimes, because they are fearful of the new experience, they need suggestion and encouragement to take the first step, but once having made a beginning they will find it enjoyable and continue coming.

One should, as far as possible, make musical experiences for children creative, even at so early an age, therefore one would start by giving them music and letting them respond to it in their own way. If the teacher can play the piano, guitar, violin or any other instrument, she can play music for the children, and if she gets no reaction from the children she can simply invite them to dance, and would expect them to react in different ways. She would not expect them all to walk, all to run, all to skip to the music she plays for them, whatever it might be. One would expect children to be as different in their creation of movement as they are in their creative work in any other medium. Very many young children have a different rhythmic reaction from that of adults, and therefore we must allow them to create their own rhythmic patterns within the adult rhythm presented to them, and *not* expect them merely to follow an adult-imposed rhythm. If one studies children's rhythmic reactions carefully when they are free to respond in their own way, one will find that a child's strong beat may come midway or two-thirds of the way between two adult strong beats. They do not correspond, but the child's will fall into a strong rhythmic pattern of its own. Therefore by imposing rigid adult rhythms on the child we are destroying his own natural creations of rhythmic patterns which are very strong at this stage.

Naturally as he gets older he will become more and more conditioned to adults' patterns of music and will probably conform to them as he does to other accepted modes of behaviour, but if he is left free in the early stages one will find his ready acceptance of more mature patterns will involve extensions of them in his own characteristic patterns of behaviour. The teacher will then give her children music, played by herself, if possible, but also using gramophone records and tape recordings whereby a much wider range of music can be given to the children. The music, after they have danced freely, may suggest some object or some piece of work they have done and a child may suggest that they dance that particular theme. If no suggestions come from the children the teacher may start them off by suggesting a theme which is closely related to some work or play that has been going on in the classroom. A picture that has been painted or some phantasy play may provide the theme. Once she has made this relationship clear to them they are more likely to come up with ideas of their own. An object in the classroom like a scarf, or a ball, or a feather, or a branch of leaves may provide the impetus for a new dance, but it must be an experience which the children have assimilated thoroughly before they can recreate it in a different medium. The teacher must provide as many varied experiences as she can as individual children will react to some stimuli more strongly than to others. Thus sometimes percussion only is satisfying to the children. Sometimes singing involves them in body movement as well as in a song. Sometimes reading good rhythmic poetry, although they may not understand the words, will evolve beautiful movements from them. Sometimes the children need a starting point to extend their experiences ; sometimes they produce their own, but the teacher must always be flexible, ready to accept a lead when it is strong enough and seems to satisfy their needs of the moment, but at other times ready to step in and enrich and widen and deepen their experiences so that they do not become abortive, frustrating and boring.

As the children go on creating movement to music they will become more accustomed *really* to listen to music, an ability which some of them have already lost because they have been surrounded by a barrage of noise in their own homes to which no one listens. When they are ready to listen without movement of their own, it will be evident to the teacher from the relaxed way in which the children respond. Therefore every now and again one would suggest that the children just listen, and if the right response does not come, it is apparent that they are not yet ready for this experience. Inevitably one will find that the children will sing and dance the topical popular music to which some of them are conditioned in their homes. One must just accept this when it happens, but at the same time we must give them such a wealth of " permanent " music that they will find it deeply satisfying and rewarding. However, as in all other activities, the teacher must herself like the music she makes for them, otherwise she will never get a wholehearted response from them. Taking music with very young children is a most rewarding experience for the teacher. The fresh and unexpected reactions of children in this field, if they are left to develop in their own way individually, is a never-failing delight. Many young teachers are afraid of taking music, because they themselves are not musically accomplished, but they need not be if they leave it to the children to lead them.

These group activities are important to the children in providing them with opportunities to further their social development through a larger teacher-directed group when they are ready for it. Through them they can learn that their enjoyment can be heightened by participation with others in any given experience and also learn gradually and perhaps unconsciously that individuals can each contribute something particular and peculiar to themselves for the enjoyment of all. This is the beginning of real community sharing. One would be aware at the same time that although these experiences are important, they are not as essential as the individual teaching and education that is going on all day in the Nursery School.

In all the other routine work the wise teacher will follow the pattern set by a good mother in her own home as far as is possible. That is, she will regard each child as an individual. She will recognise at milk time and at meal times that each child has individual tastes in food and in rates of eating. This is not a time when she will expect conformity of behaviour from all her children as they have all been differently conditioned by their early experiences at home. It is true that because children of this age are very imitative, they will follow one another's leads so that a certain amount of conformity will prevail, but there are always individuals who will stand out from the general pattern. Some of the children have had difficulties over weaning, or have mothers who are over-anxious about their children's feeding, and this has set up in the children feelings of anxiety and hostility to all food.

These anxieties are further exacerbated by the strange environment, by the insecurity of not knowing how the teacher will react to any given pattern of behaviour, and by the large numbers of children all feeding at the same time. Therefore the child must be free to choose how much food he will have and what kinds of food he will have from the range offered to him. Obviously the teacher will give him every encouragement and suggest that he tries something, but the ultimate choice must be his. He must never be forced to eat. If he is, he will not be able to digest it properly because of his emotional disturbance, and we shall be setting up even more antagonism to food as a whole, or particular foods, which may persist all through his life. As the child finds that no one is cross with him for his rejection of food and that his wishes are respected, he will gradually conform to the behaviour patterns of the other children. If he persists in the rejection of food and is continually emotionally upset for a fairly long period, it would probably mean that this child is not yet ready for the complexities of Nursery School life and would be better at home with his mother. One of the advantages of the part-time Nursery School is the fact that children do not have to eat their food away from their mothers. It is after all the most important experience of their day and should be shared with the person they love best and with whom they feel most secure.

The same pattern of procedure should be followed over sleep routines. Here again the children are wholly individual in their need for sleep. Some need a lot of sleep and some none at all, and a child who is *made* to sleep will not gain much value from it because of the emotional disturbance that will accompany it. We must remember that many small children, particularly when they are new to school, are afraid that if they do go to sleep and their mothers come they might go away without them. Also for those of them who have had hospital experience, which is always painful and distressing, the two situations are too much alike and may involve the same fear and apprehension. Therefore the going to bed must be made as enjoyable as possible. Children should not be made to lie down immediately, be tucked up tightly in blankets and told to go to sleep. It should be a very gradual process. They should be allowed to take a soft toy to bed with them if they like, preferably one they have brought from home, so that the home image is still with them. They should be allowed to sit up on their beds at first and gradually be encouraged to lie down. A frightened child should be allowed to sit up as long as he likes and never forced to lie down. Again, as with eating, most of the children are ready to relax, lie down and be comfortable as they are tired after a long morning's activities, and so one gets a general conformity of behaviour.

Some children, however, will never sleep, and therefore one must make provision for them to get up after about half an hour. There is little possibility that they will fall asleep after that period, but they will have had a rest. If possible, a room should be kept free where they may go and play quietly, possibly have a story time with one of the assistants. If no separate room is available, sometimes a corridor or cloakroom can be utilised, and if the worst comes to the worst a corner of the room where the other children are sleeping can be used. Once children are really asleep, it takes a great deal of noise to wake them up. When the weather is fine, of course, they can go into the garden and play. A child who sleeps on after the other children are all up, through all the noise and disturbance of the Nursery, obviously needs the sleep and should be allowed to sleep on in a corner of the room until his mother comes for him. Where a child has to be woken, it should be done very gently, as children are often dazed with sleep and frightened at waking up in a strange place. Whenever a child is frightened or distressed physical contact with an adult helps him to recover, so the teacher would take the child on her lap and let him come to gradually. Physical contact is the best way of conveying to the child the sense of security and love that he needs so badly.

All through the day, education in such things as toilet training (which must be individual), washing hands and face and combing hair, are going on. The children are also learning to take their place in society by helping to clear up the toys they have been using, sweeping up the sand, mopping up the water, caring for the flowers and animals on the nature table, and helping to get out beds and put them away again. All these experiences are exciting and interesting to them, and when the first excitement of doing these things has waned, they will have developed the habit of helping to clear up after themselves. One cannot, however, hold such young children wholly responsible for any such activity. They always need the adult's help to carry it through successfully to the end, and one would set a high standard for such work. The teacher should always finish off properly herself, never leaving a half-finished job. As teachers, we are setting standards for life, and the higher we set those standards the more the children will try to live up to them.

Nursery School education must never attempt to be a substitute for the home ; it must always be complementary. As far as possible it should approximate to the environment of a good home, always taking into account the fact of having much larger numbers of children of the same age. It has, of course, great advantages of giving children real space to play in and a great deal of equipment, which is either too large or too expensive for the ordinary home. It is, however, not essential for all children to attend Nursery Schools and to some it may do more harm than good. A child of about three-and-a-half to five can profit a great deal from all the experiences that he finds in a Nursery School for two or three hours a day, but where he has a good home with a garden, with the ordinary play materials such as I have described, and the possibility of playing with two or three friends of about his own age, he is better at home in the love and security of his mother and his family.

Bibliography

BOWLBY, J. *Child Care and the Growth of Love.* Pelican Books, 1953.

BOWLEY, A. H. *The Problem of Family Life.* E. S. Livingstone, 1948.

BRIDGES, K. M. B. *Social and Emotional Development of the Pre-school Child.* Kegan Paul, Trench, Trubner & Co. Ltd., 1931.

BUHLER, CHARLOTTE. *From Birth to Maturity.* Kegan Paul, Trench, Trubner & Co. Ltd., 1937.

BUHLER, CHARLOTTE, and HETZER, HILDEGARDE. *Testing Children's Development from Birth to School Age.* Farrar & Rinehart, 1939.

FLUGEL, J. C. *The Psycho-analytic Study of the Family.* Hogarth Press, 1939.

GARDNER, D. BRUCE. *Development in Early Childhood.* Harper & Row, 1964.

GESELL, AMATRUDA, CASTNER, and THOMPSON. *Biographies of Child Development.* Hamish Hamilton, 1939.

GESELL, A. and ILG, FRANCES L. *Child Development, an Introduction to the Study of Human Growth.* Harper, 1944.

GESELL, A. *The First Five Years of Life.* Harper, 1940.

GOODENOUGH, F. L. *Measurement of Intelligence by Drawings.* World Book Co., 1926.

ISAACS, SUSAN. *The Nursery Years.* Routledge, 1932.

ISAACS, SUSAN. *Social Development of Young Children.* Routledge, 1937.

ISAACS, SUSAN. *Intellectual Growth in Young Children.* Routledge, 1930.

LEWIS, M. M. *How Children Learn to Speak.* New York, Basic Books, 1939.

PIAGET, JEAN. *The Language and Thought of the Child.* Harcourt, Brace, 1926.

PIAGET, JEAN. *Judgement and Reasoning in the Child.* Harcourt, Brace, 1928.

TANNER, J. M. *Education and Physical Growth.* University of London Press, 1961.

WALL, W. D. *Education and Mental Health.* George G. Harrap & Co. Ltd., 1955.

GREY, WALTER W. *The Living Brain.* Duckworth, 1953.

WATTS, A. F. *The Language and Mental Development of Children.* Harrap, 1944.

Index

137

Date Due